WISDOM FROM THE PULPIT

A Collection of 80 Short Walks

In Everyday Life

FATHER GEORGE McKENNA

CMJ

Marian Publishers

Soul Assurance Prayer Plan

Published by CMJ Marian Publishers and Distributors
Post Office Box 661
Oak Lawn, Illinois 60454
http://www.cmjbooks.com
jwby@aol.com
Phone: 708-636-2995
Fax: 708-636-2855

Father McKenna's previously published work's:
I'll Only Speak for 3 Minutes series are no longer
available.

Graphics:
    Pete Massari
    Rockford, IL 61114

Format & Editing:
    Stratum Concepts,
    Oak Lawn, IL 60453

    Christina Sullivan
    Libertyville, Illinois 60048

    Curtin Originals
    Crown Point, IN 46307

ISBN# 1-891280-59-7
Library of Congress # applied for

To all the Chicago Midway Airport Chapel volunteer workers, past and present, for their enthusiastic help and complete dedication.

18th Anniversary of Midway Airport

ABOUT THE AUTHOR

Father George McKenna is founder of the chapel at Midway Airport, and author of the well-known volume series, I'll Only Speak For 3 Minutes.

At the time of this printing, Father is still celebrating Mass at the Midway chapel. He now resides in a community with fellow priests who have become a blessing for him.

All requests for information on Father should be directed to CMJ Marian Publishers. Please keep Father, and all priests, in your prayers.

CMJ Marian Publishers
PO Box 661
Oak Lawn, IL 60454
Tel: 708-636-2995

The Inside Story of Midway Chapel
By Father George McKenna

One cold January day, while sitting in the terminal of Midway Airport, I said to myself, "Wouldn't it be a good thing if religious services could be held somewhere here? It is now 1987 and not one religious service has been held at the airport since its opening in 1927."

I put this possibility before Padre Pio, whom I had admired from the early days of my priesthood. As a Capuchin monk in Italy, he had inspired so many people with his strong faith in the Mass and Eucharist. In the history of the Catholic Church, Padre Pio has been the only priest bearing the stigmata of all five wounds of Christ.

A year before the Midway Chapel was to open, I found myself at a house for priests, the Foyer

Sacerdotal, in Paris. At dinner, a French priest came and sat next to me for the three evenings he spent there. On the third night, an American priest asked this French priest what kind of work he did. His answer stunned me, "I am Father Andre. I am in charge of promoting the cause of Padre Pio for sainthood in all France."

He went on to tell me, through our American interpreter, that he had known Padre Pio well and had gone regularly for Confession to this holy man. From his station wagon, he gave me photos of Pio, who had died in1968. I promised Padre Pio that we would always have his photo in our airport chapel if he brought about its opening. We have kept our promise. He has since been canonized a saint.

In 1987 and the first months of 1988, the people of Our Lady of the Snows Parish prayed for the opening of the Chapel. As an associate pastor in the parish, I had shared my dream with them.

At this same time, I visited a parish friend dying of cancer, Bill Sikon. As we sat together, he wrote on a piece of paper, "Chapel, how does it look?" I said, "When you get into Heaven, you will have to pray for us." He died within the week. Would Bill be working for us in Heaven.

A few days later there was a breakthrough. Mr. Bill Krystiniak, the alderman of our airport ward, became a key person in dealing with the City of Chicago's Department of Aviation. Without him, we would have made little progress in convincing others of the need for a chapel in the airport.

Even after Cardinal Bernadin and city officials gave their permission for Mass to be held in Midway Airport, no one could find a place for the Chapel. After months of effort and prayer, the people in Our Lady of the Snows were offering their difficulties to God for its opening.

Under the direction of David Hinson, Midway Airport came up with a generous offer. They gave us the use of one gate on Saturday evening and Sunday mornings.

After all these years, we continue to pray at every Mass for the airlines and the health of their employees and all airport workers who have shown the chapel workers a courteous and helpful spirit.

At the first Mass in Midway Airport on July 24, 1988, a young woman guitarist, Erin Solkowski from Our Lady of the Snows Parish, accompanied the overflowing congregation in song. This was her only visit to the airport chapel, and no one else has ever played a musical instrument in the celebration of our Masses.

Later, Erin's mother told me an amazing story. Erin's middle name is Pio, given at birth. Ann Solkowski, during a difficult delivery, prayed to Padre Pio promising that she would name the child Pio. Erin was delivered safely. Padre Pio was saying that first Mass in the airport, "See, I am with you." Thank you, Padre Pio.

A Late Age Disclosure

These days, people are coming "out of the closet", as it were, to tell of their hidden lifestyles. So, at 87, I will do the same. I must confess I have fallen deeply in love with a beautiful woman in Paris, France. We both agree that it was love at first sight. We communicate often, but not by E-mail. I have her picture in my room and think of her often during the day.

When I'm in Paris, I visit her elegant home overlooking the Seine River every day. My friend welcomes me warmly and the hours slip away like minutes. I can share my closest thoughts with her. Highly intelligent, she gives me new insights into my wonderment about life and its mysteries.

In the past when young people in love told me that they were walking on air, I smiled to myself. Now, the shoe is on the other foot. Since I met this charming woman, I find life glorious, and everyone I meet, special. Her friendship has changed my life for the better.

My friend does not have a French name. She is Mary, also called the Mother of Christ. In Paris, she lives in the magnificent Notre Dame Cathedral. Yes, this is the woman I fell in love with. Every day, thousands of her friends pour through the front doors to kneel at her feet as she stands on a pedestal in the sanctuary. With loving concern, Mary, my beautiful friend, looks down on these people of all nations. Often I have knelt before Her in poor spirits and went away in love with life.

In the summer, we can all fall deeply in love with Mary, the Mother of Christ. Plan to set up a shrine that we can pray before, a painting, a statue. Notice the gracious way of living in her Son, Jesus of Nazareth. In His first visit to His   after   the

Resurrection, He could have rightly fired all of them, except John. But Instead, He approached them with ways of love, forgiveness, kindness, encouragement, and greetings of peace. Later, the disciples died for Him.

As a child, Jesus learned these gracious qualities at His Mother's knee. We too, can bring these ways of living into our lives by kneeling at Mary's knees. She will, in her love for each of us, gladly build up a burning desire in us to possess these gracious gifts.

Notre Dame Cathedral in Paris, France

A Valiant Women

Some time ago, we celebrated the Mass of the Resurrection for Lily McNicholas, a friend from where I formerly lived. Only then did we discover the heroic things Lily had done as a nurse in the British army in World War II. It happened in the English Channel when an enemy submarine torpedoed a Dutch hospital ship that Lily was serving on.

As the ship began to sink, Lily gave up her seat in her life boat to an immobile soldier. No need to ask why. She did it without hesitation. As the ship began its final plunge, Lily slid down the broad side into the water. Not able to swim, she depended on her life jacket for survival. In the midst of all this havoc, Lily came upon a one legged soldier, struggling to keep stable in the water. Again, without hesitation, she grabbed hold of him to keep him from drowning. After many hours, a rescue ship picked them out of the water with Lily's hair bleached white from the salt water. For her heroic act above the call of duty, the King of England bestowed the Order of the Empire Medal on Lily McNicholas.

One word in the dictionary describes Lily's state of mind. She had the gift of maturity, the ability to live in some-one else's world. In the Gospel, Jesus saw a fig tree not bearing fruit over a period of time. It had not matured! The Master said, "Cut it down!" I must mature, that is, grow up to be unselfish, and conscious of the needs of others before my own. Only then will I bear fruit! Young Lily McNicholas was willing to die that others might live.

Some nights, as I look over the happenings of my day, I am sad when I see how completely I was taken up with my own concerns, comforts, and with little thought for the needs of others. How immature on my part! Is not sin a sign of immaturity? In sin, I choose my own selfish needs and turn from God. At Lily's Funeral Mass, I resolved to forget my own fears and anxieties and think of others.

A Sabbath-Keeper, A Person Of Wisdom

In Jerusalem, I have often witnessed the beginning of the Sabbath on Friday evenings at sundown. A startling change comes over the whole City, as buses, taxis and traffic disappear from the streets. Without exception, all shops and factories close down until sunset on Saturday evening, the end of the Sabbath. A peaceful silence, a stillness, fell upon the deserted boulevards.

On Friday evenings, from my location outside the walls of the Old City, I saw wave after wave of Jewish Sabbath-Keepers, walking up a steep hill on a six lane highway, towards the Old City on their way to the Wailing Wall. Dressed in their best and in a somber mood, these religious people would begin their Sabbath with prayers at this Holy Place, located in the Jewish Quarter of the Old City. The Jews consider the Wailing Wall to be the West Wall of the Temple, from the time of Christ.

After these experiences, I would come home to the United States with a desire to give more attention to the way I celebrate the Christian Sabbath on Sundays. God rested on the 7th day, not because He needed this, but rather to give us a message. "Give yourselves a rest from the busyness of life and think of Me." In the American culture, there is no hope of imitating the Sabbath of Jerusalem in regards to shutting down all activities. However, as individuals, we can bring everything to a halt in our hearts and spirits. In peace, we can pass the day!

The Sunday Sabbath rest gives us a chance to think of what we are doing with our lives. A good beginning is to worship God at Mass and receive His Sacred Body and Blood. Avoid shopping on this special day. Manual work, like washing clothes, housework, and cutting the lawn will pull us away from the spirit of the day. We meet our family's needs, but we reserve some private time for ourselves. Look forward with delight to the Sabbath!

Solitude, prayer, Bible reading, quiet reflections on the ideals of Christ, and even writing down our thoughts in a journal, can give a rewarding Sabbath time. Sabbath-Keepers will spend this time in quiet joy. In the Gospels, the writers tell us of Jesus retreating to the mountain tops for prayer. He felt a desperate need to commune with His Heavenly Father to complete His work! He also kept the Sabbath by attending the synagogue services.

By wearing our best or near best clothes, we can deepen our sense of reverence for the Sabbath. Even in Summer, refuse to follow the deplorable trend of shorts, overalls, sandals, etc. in Church.

Father George McKenna

The Wailing Wall in Jerusalem

Make Your Home A Suburb Of Heaven

Several weeks ago, I received a surprise letter from a woman whose marriage I had witnessed twenty years ago. I remember a line I had spoken in the homily at her wedding Mass. *"Make your home a suburb of Heaven."* The first time I had ever used this idea. A year later, she came back to me and said, *"We have tried to make our home a suburb of Heaven."* Usually, brides and grooms seldom hear anything the priests say at their Nuptial Masses.

My letter-writing friend went on to say, *"I remember a sermon you once gave while I was at St. Barnabas, which I carry with me and repeat to myself and to others, and to my children (now adults), often. On a Sunday, set aside as a Day of*

Prayer for World Peace, you proposed a question. Why would not God grant such a prayer? After all, peace is something good for which to ask. Your answer is what has stuck in my head, and what has influenced my behavior for years. You said that perhaps God could not grant such a prayer, because peace is something which each individual person must make a part of his or her life, in the way in which he or she addresses life and those who cross his or her path. You said that love, forgiveness, reconciliation, and a desire to meet the challenge of peace within each individual is necessary to make peace. You said that God did not keep peace from us, but that we, each and every one, kept peace from our lives in our inability to reconcile the differences that separated each of us from some other."

How pleasant to have been quoted after a period of twenty years. Evidently, my friend has made peace a prized goal in life for herself and her family.

The prophets called Jesus the Prince of Peace since peace made up His chief ministry. By dying on the cross, He reconciled all people to His Father. He brought harmony to earth with His words, "Love one another as I have loved you. Love God with all your strength and your neighbor as yourself."

Of all gifts of God in life, peace ranks first. A heart free of ill will, resentments, unresolved angers, and hatred provide a perfect breeding ground for the virtues that make for holiness like love, gentleness, patience and joy. When a nation enjoys peace, all the works of the spirit (paintings, sculptures, writings and works of charity) thrive and flourish. A home filled with gentle words, forgiving attitudes and true love makes a "Suburb of Heaven," because peace abides there.

No Happiness In Sin

The First Reading and the Gospel give the theme for the Mass: God forgives sin. He not only forgives, but forgets them afterwards.

St. John Bosco (1815 - 1888), a favorite Saint of mine, the Apostle of Youth, often told his students, *"There is no happiness in sin,"* that is, in the breaking of God's Commandments. This motto helped me often during life. Call the Commandments, *"The Guidelines To Happiness."* Sin can look attractive, an immediate answer to a present problem, but once swallowed, it leaves our hearts in unrest and darkness.

St. Augustine, a serious sinner in his early life, put it well. In speaking to God, he said, *"My soul is restless until it rests in Thee.*" How providential, on the part of Christ, to give us agents, His priests, the power to forgive sins. The priest can say with absolute certainty, *"Your sins are forgiven you. Your soul is in perfect condition."* No long drawn out process required.

We can ask millions of our fellow Americans in prison, *"Did sinning bring you freedom or a life behind bars?"* The answer is quite evident. Even, if we, as sinners, do not end up in a public prison, we become dissatisfied with life. Our hearts are in the prison of darkness of spirit. After 63 years as a priest, I have never met a happy sinner. Only hearts filled with heavy sadness, especially in case of serious sins.

As a priest, I have always found hearing confession to be the most satisfying ministry, apart from offering Mass. As a sinner myself, with many faults, my heart is always with the persons confessing their sins. I know that I am bringing happiness to them as they hope to begin a new way of life. If they have been away from confession for a long time, I assure them that I need no numbers, no details, no questions asked...just a general statement about the Commandments broken.

Scripture says, "I, God, do not remember your sins." God wants us to do the same for ourselves. Approach the priest with confidence. Hear the priest say, "Your soul is in perfect condition, like your baptismal day."

A Powerful Story

One day a teacher asked her students to list the names of the other students in the room on two sheets of paper, leaving a space between each name. Then she told them to think of the nicest thing they could say about each of their classmates and write it down. It took the remainder of the class period to finish their assignment.

As the students left the classroom, each one handed in the papers. That Saturday, the teacher wrote down the name of each student on a separate sheet of paper and listed what everyone else had said about that individual. On Monday, she gave each student his or her list. Before long, the entire class was smiling. *"Really,"* she heard whispered,

"I never knew I meant anything to anyone," and *"I didn't know others liked me so much,"* were most of the comments. No one ever mentioned those papers in class again.

She never knew if they discussed them after class or with their parents, but it didn't matter. The exercise had accomplished its purpose. The students were happy with themselves and each other. That group of students moved on.

Several years later, one of the students was killed in Vietnam and his teacher attended the funeral. She had never seen a serviceman in a military coffin. He looked so handsome, so mature. The church was packed. The teacher was the last one to bless the coffin.

As she stood there, one of the soldiers who acted as pallbearer approached her. *"Were you Mark's math teacher?"* he asked. She nodded, *"yes"*. Then he said, *"Mark talked a lot about you."* At the luncheon, Mark's mother and father were there, obviously waiting to speak with his teacher. *"We want to show you something,"* his father said, taking a wallet out of his pocket.

He carefully removed two worn pieces of notebook paper that had obviously been taped, folded and refolded many times. On the paper were listed all the good things each of Mark's classmates had said about him. *"Thank you so much for doing that,"* Mark's mother said. *"As you can see, Mark treasured it. They found this on Mark when he was killed."*

Nancy Fuccillo, wife of Captain Ron Fucillo. She teaches 6th Grade in a Catholic School in Lebanon, Illinois.

The Best Is Yet To Come

Twenty-five years ago, I found myself in Paris at prayer in the Chapel of my residence. My spirits had never been so low after leaving a troublesome assignment. At age 63, the adventure of Priesthood appeared over. I had taken a six month leave of absence to regroup myself. Suddenly, in the twilight of that evening in the Chapel, I pictured the Risen Christ standing in the sanctuary much as He came to His disciples on the shores of the Sea of Galilee to raise their spirits.

I heard Him say, *"George, how goes it?"* In surprise, I blurted out, *"Lord, I need three H's...a Home, Hope and Health."* Several months later, my prayers were answered. I came to a little parish down the street from Midway Airport. I lived in a little cottage, alone, a real Home. The kindness and the love of the people gave me new Hope for good things to come. In my walks around the perimeter of Midway Airport, new Health came to me. On retiring at the compulsory age of 70 in 1988, I decided, with the help of volunteers from the parish, to open a Catholic Chapel in the airport.

The present Midway Airport opened in 1927 and up until 1988, no religious service had ever been offered in its confines. We began to offer Masses on weekends in July of 1988 in open gates, in between flights amid the frequent announcements and movement of people on the concourses. The best adventure of Priesthood was just beginning. So, life has been for past 19 years.

What looked like a disaster in Paris, 1982, turned out to be the greatest blessing of my Priesthood. Maybe, some here this morning are preparing to throw up the white towel on a forsaken marriage, the despair of a sickness, bills seemingly impossible to pay, the heartbreak of disappointment in the way others are treating us, especially our children or close friends. We might know others in the above predicaments.

Think of my story above. Picture the Risen Christ looking on and saying, *"How goes it, dear friend?"* Pour out our needs in detail to this gentle, all-loving Christ the way I did. Do this with much faith!

Alfred Lord Tennyson, the English poet, wrote, *"Come, my friends, it's not too late to seek a newer world an invitation to a world of faithful love, enduring peace and exhilarating joy."*

A Eucharistic People, A Loving People

One early morning, a while ago, on the radio, I heard a father tell a story about his son, home from college for the summer. According to the father, the young man, with his hair reaching down to his shoulders, his shirt unbuttoned and with no shoes, went to church services with his parents on a Sunday morning.

On the way home from the Church, the young man came up with a profound conclusion. With a faraway look in his eye, perhaps one of disappointment, the young man spoke quietly, *"You certainly can tell who the Christians are in Church on Sunday morning."* On his coming into the Church, some had openly rejected him, while others gave him the cold shoulder, moving away from him when he sat in their section. However, a number of people welcomed him with a smile or friendly nod of their heads.

At the Last Supper, after humbly washing the feet of His disciples, Jesus said, *"As I have done for you, so also, you do for others."* Shortly afterwards, He gave them and all to come after them the Holy Eucharist, because He knew how difficult it is to be a loving person. Perhaps the present day churches have many empty seats because modern day disciples of the Lord do not show enough of a loving spirit to the world about them.

Young people might say, *"What good does the Eucharist do? I don't see churchgoers any more charitable than those who never receive the Eucharist."* Perhaps, we do not emphasize enough to ourselves what the first effect of the Eucharist should be namely a growth in love!

We might cite a few examples of love going out to others. An auto struck a 12 year old boy on his bicycle. In the hospital he hung between life and death, so his parish called a prayer service for his well being. 700 people came to pray for the boy, a stranger to most of them.

Another example came about when a priest announced at Sunday Mass, *"Miss Virginia Lee will be buried tomorrow. She had no relatives. Since no one will be at the funeral Mass, please come if you can."* 80 parishioners came the next day for the Mass. The Eucharist should make us a loving people.

Classic Time To Express Love

Another Valentine's Day has come upon us. Hallmark Cards rejoices on such a day since people make this a big card buying occasion. Valentine's Day, named after an early saint in our Church, gives many a shy person a chance to express love and affection towards others.

Back on Valentine's Day, 1933, as an Eighth Grader in St. Theodore's School, I came to my classroom after lunch. To my surprise, I found a tiny candy heart, no bigger than a postage stamp, on my desk. Written on this precious gift were the words, *"I Love YOU."*

My boyish spirits went sky high. Someone in my class cares for me, I cried out to myself. Which one of five or six girls did this, I wondered. That didn't matter. I must be worth something. After all these years, this experience stays with me to raise my spirits and prove to me the power of those words....
"I Love You."

When victims of 9/11 were cell-phoning their last words to family members, at the end, they said, *"I Love You."* Hopefully, they had spoken those precious words many times in the past.

In the past, when friends said to me, *"I Love You,"* my shy response was, *"Oh, thank you."* I falsely thought that a priest is not supposed to say,*"I love you, too."* People might take it the wrong way. Now, with the onset of wisdom, I answer, *"I love you, too."*

In recent years, I found out the name of the classmate who was responsible for my memory of Valentine's Day in 1933. She was the sweetest, most charming girl in the class. Still alive today, she has retained all those beautiful traits.

Are we going to be miserly in the use of powerful words of joy and encouragement, even after Valentine's Day has gone by? Leave a life-long memory in the minds and hearts of struggling fellow pilgrims with the sincere use of those life changing words, *"I Love You."*

In conclusion, I love all my readers for taking time to bring the above message into their hearts. Life might never be the same.

The Jabez Prayer

An unusual book, *The Prayer Of Jabez,* has been in the top ten best selling non-fiction books for 54 weeks. At present, 10 million copies have been sold. Frankly, *The Prayer Of Jabez,* (pronounced JabZEz), has added new excitement and adventure to my spiritual life. About 2 months ago, a friend sent me a copy, opening for me a new door to the Mystery of God. I say the prayer several times a day, with a strong emphasis on my faith in it.

The man, Jabez, was only mentioned once in Scripture, in the *1st Book of Chronicles*, the least read book in the Old Testament. It is the least read because the Book only contains a long list of names. In these Chronicles, the Sacred Writer suddenly stops listing names and says Jabez stood out as an honorable man, above all others of his time.

The author of *The Prayer Of Jabez,* Bruce Wilkinson, an outstanding minister in the United States was a dynamic speaker who heard of the *Jabez Prayer* some 30 years ago in a lecture. Bruce concluded that Jabez succeeded because of the way he prayed. From that day on, Bruce began saying the prayer every day. Startling things began to happen in his ministry. *The Prayer Of Jabez* follows, with a few words of explanation.

"Lord, that You would bless me indeed." We consider ourselves selfish if we prayed that way. No! God wants us to ask for blessings. We will miss out on many blessings if we don't ask for them. In Scripture, the word, *"indeed,"* is equal to five exclamation marks(!!!!!).

"That you would enlarge my territory." Show me, Lord, ways I can increase my ministry of spreading your Kingdom on earth. Send people to

me so that I can help them. Your blessings will make me more capable. *"That Your Hand would be with me."* The word, *"hand,"* signifies the power and strength of God. Without Your help, I can accomplish nothing.

"That You would keep me from evil lest I cause pain"... Watch over me, lest I expose myself needlessly to the wiles of Satan. And the Sacred Writer concludes, *"God heard his prayer and granted him his wishes."*

The Little Donkeys Of The Lord

On the first Palm Sunday, Jesus entered Jerusalem with His Good News, on the back of a lowly donkey, the least attractive and appealing of all animals. He could have come on a white charger. Christ calls all of us, not just some of us, to be His disciples, that is, carriers of Him and His Good news to the city. We, His followers, can be His little donkeys in this magnificent work, with all our weaknesses and deficiencies. No need to beg off with excuses. The Lord will make up for what we lack.

Mother Teresa of Calcutta required three qualities of those entering her religious order; to be a loving person, to have enthusiasm for life, and to be a cheerful follower of Christ. To be little donkeys of Christ, we need these, too. Prayer and study can make these qualities ours.

What is the Good News? God loves us. God has a personal love for each one of us. God wants to walk with us in life, to help and support us. God sent His only son to be like us and save us from sin.

As disciples of the Lord, we need not preach in public on soap boxes or go door to door evangelizing. No! Just be ourselves. Loving, in that we are willing to sacrifice ourselves for others. Enthusiastic, in that we see life as a glorious and thrilling adventure, and cheerful towards life and its happenings, like saying, *"Ho hum, my family is falling apart. I just lost my job. I go for surgery next week. I know God will help me through all this. There is a song in my heart."* Think LEC!

Our family members will need no preaching! Our example will speak for itself! We can bring them closer to God. Our co-workers and people in our community will be asking us how they can bring

LEC into their lives. Be willing to give all time in their inquiries about our religious beliefs. We all can be little donkeys for the Lord, carrying Him and His Good News to the city. This could be an interesting and thrilling adventure in our present day.

Be generous in sharing books and articles with others. If the time is proper, tell others the names of good movies, TV shows, or radio programs. Think LEC: love, enthusiasm, and cheerfulness. Daily prayer is necessary to keep these qualities alive in our hearts.

Jerusalem in October of 2005

Struggle Brings Strength

A few years ago, in the mid-afternoon, I entered a huge cathedral-like Church in London, England, called Brompton's Oratory. Here, the saintly John Cardinal Newman worked and lived in the 19th Century. The organist was practicing a difficult piece of music on the Church's mighty pipe organ, pouring forth glorious sounds.

Now and then, he would stop and repeat himself so that he could perfect his execution of a certain score of notes. He wasn't satisfied with himself. I could see the organist, high in the balcony, hunched over over the keyboard and exerting much effort to touch all the notes. He was truly struggling with this masterpiece of music to bring out its true beauty.

We, too, struggle with our unruly nature to make ourselves masterpieces of God's creation, fully mature people with our lives patterned after the Life of Christ. The big victory in life lies in the conquest of our very own selves.

In our hearts, we find the battlefield where we wrestle with our selfishness and weakness. If I yearn to be a better person, more like Christ, then the soil of my heart will be excellent ground for God's messages this Eastertime.

When I was younger, I thought that, at my present age, life would be wrapped up in neat little packages. However, I find that I am still struggling with my own selfish tendencies. But, this has been the most exciting part of life, fighting to make myself a better person, one capable of offering glorious music to the world.

A woman about to give birth, struggles to bring forth the child within her, but how rewarding for herself, her family, and the world. *"Create in me a clean heart, Oh Lord."* Read the lives of great people and how they became geniuses through hard work and daily effort.

That afternoon in the Brompton Oratory, convinced me I could only find victory over my unruly inclinations through daily prayer and closeness to the Risen Christ.

Jerusalem, October, 2005

On October 4th, 2005, our party of six, two priests and four lay people, came to the Old City of Jerusalem, not as sightseers, but as pilgrims seeking the face of Christ. We desired most of all to bring the Spirit of Christ into our lives, His meekness, humility, and His spirit of prayer. We resided at the First Station of the Cross with the Sisters of Sion, in the heart of the Old City. The courtyard of Pilate lay in the sub-level of the building.

Everyday, we concelebrated Mass at some holy place in Jerusalem and its environs along with two priests from Ireland, a blessed happening for our group. In their early 70s, former missionaries in Africa, these two men shared much with us about life there. Our meals together came to be a daily joy and a foretelling of the happiness of the heavenly banquet awaiting us. It was twelve days of blissful living for all of us.

On the first morning, we walked the Way of the Cross to the Church of the Holy Sepulcher to offer Mass in an inner Chapel. Crowds of pilgrims, the first in five years, filled this holy place, a sign of some peace in the troubled Mid-East. The next day brought us to the Garden of Gethsemane, just a twenty minute walk outside the walls of the Old City. Here, in Mary's Grotto, a cave-like place, the words of the Mass told us of the Betrayal of Christ by Judas. Sin took on a new meaning for us, its ugliness laid bare.

Our group walked about the Old City, to Cenacle Chapel, some fifty feet from the site of the Last Supper, to Veronica's home at the Sixth Station where we offered Mass in the Chapel. All the while, the wisdom of being a prayerful person was sinking into our hearts. After all, Christ was becoming more and more real to us. He actually lived here.

One morning, we traveled to Bethany, the former home of the sisters Martha and Mary and their brother, Lazarus, for a peaceful Mass. We prayed for the spirit of hospitality this family had shown Christ. At Emmaus, where the Risen Christ met the two despairing disciples, the Scripture at Mass reminded us that Jesus always walks with us in our sorrows and darkness. At Bethlehem, we offered Mass in the Field of the Shepherds in a cave-like Chapel. How peaceful!

We spent two days in Galilee, 85 miles north of Jerusalem, with Masses in the Basilica of the Annunciation and on the shore of the Sea of Galilee, site of the miraculous multiplication of bread. Included were a boat ride on the Sea of Galilee, and a drive to the top of Mt. Tabor.

The Road of Life

Mt. Thabor, the Mount of the Transfiguration, rises 1000 feet over the surrounding plains in Galilee, close to Nazareth. Think of the Sears Tower in downtown Chicago. I remember my first visit to this wondrous place, in the Summer of 1959. My three priest companions and I stayed overnight on this mountain top in the Franciscan monastery. I recall perfect silence that evening except for the moaning of the wind. In the plains below, the lights of the small communities shone like jewels. This mountain was a perfect place for prayer!

Because of the steepness of the slopes, only one road meanders to the top. See the aerial graphic to the right on this page. Notice the road twisting and

and burning, zig-zagging right and left as it makes its way to the top! This road gives us a picture of life. In our efforts to see and be with the Glorified Christ, we must go through these zig-zags. This is the only road!

In these twists and turns on the road of life, we often begin to wonder, "Am I on the right road to seeing the Lord in His Glory? Is there some other highway I can take and avoid this corkscrew road?" No, there isn't!

What are these zig-zags on the Glory Road? We can make up a long litany of disappointments heartaches, personal failures, hurts from close friends, physical sicknesses, problems in married life, trials in raising a family, financial woes, and grief for departed loved ones.

As I write this, a telephone message tells me of a young friend who was called back to the hospital because of her worsening condition. She wants to live for her two small boys and bring the message of

Mary to her community. She, too, wonders if she is on the Glory Road. Yes, she is!

Many reading this article nod in agreement that they, too, are going through many sharp twists and turns on the Glory Road. They wonder if they are losing out in their efforts to see the glorified Christ as the three disciples saw Him on Mt. Thabor. St. Paul wrote from a prison cell, *"Stand firm in the Lord."* In other words persevere and refuse to give up! How do we stand firm in the Lord? By praying to Him every day, throwing ourselves on His Love and Mercy, and by offering up our pain and suffering to God in union with the sufferings of Christ on the cross.

Mt. Thabor (aerial view). Mountain of the Transfiguration

A Meeting At Bethlehem

One cold, rainy, gusty February morning, a *"cheroot,"* or jitney cab, took me on the five mile trip from Jerusalem to about a mile from Bethlehem. A "cheroot" picks up people along the road. The cost is two shekels, or about 75 cents.

After an exhausting hike up a steep road, I arrived at the Church of the Nativity for my 9:30 am Mass in the Grotto. Most scholars agree that Mary gave birth to the Messiah near this location. My celebration of Mass, one on Christmas Day, lifted my spirits and helped me forget the cold, penetrating dampness.

After Mass, I gave an offering for a handful of slim, wax tapers to light at the Grotto, reached by descending a flight of stone steps. A man next to me, a complete stranger, asked me where to obtain the candles. I offered him half of what I had. He took the seven tapers and said, *"how much?"* I shook my head, indicating *"no charge"* and gave no further thought to the incident.

That night, to my surprise, this *"stranger"* sat across the table from me in our Franciscan Hospice in Jerusalem. In the following days, Dennis Croffield joined our little group as I offered Mass at the Holy Places in and around Jerusalem. None of us knew each other a few days before this.

Dennis turned out to be a top flight artist from London, England. Distraught with life, he had come to the Holy Land to find some peace of heart. On my departure day, he gave me a copy of his latest book entitled, *English Cathedrals.* I suppose, in thanks for the little tapers I gave him in Bethlehem. The book contains his charcoal drawings of 18 Cathedrals in England.

As we invest in the welfare of others, even complete strangers, we never know what the outcome will be. Jesus rode into Jerusalem on Palm Sunday on the back of a donkey. He was investing in each one of us, strangers, not yet born.

What will we repay Him, for His grand act of unselfishness? Will we, as Dennis had done to me, surprise Christ with a total giving of ourselves to His Honor and Glory?

Bethlehem Square in the Holy Land

A Grateful Person Cherishes God

In June, 1959, I visited the Shrine of Our Lady at Lourdes, France, for the first time. As I walked into the main Church, Our Lady of the Rosary, my eyes caught sight of the great number of markings on its walls. Each tile plaque, about the size of the license plate on our autos, had one large word written on it, *"Merci"* (the French word for *"thanks"*). Underneath this was the name of a person or family and a date at the bottom.

These plaques covered the walls from the floors almost to the ceilings. Through the intercession of Mary, people in need had received favors from God. In their gratitude, they wished to give thanks for Mary's help in a public way. All these markings of

"Merci" impressed me with Mary's power and willingness to help us in our desperate times. I saw too, how gratitude was a fitting response to these favors given. Through the Rosary, miracles of healing had come to all these people. During my tenth pilgrimage to Lourdes two years ago, the *"Merci's"* still overwhelmed me!

In fantasy, how wonderful it would be if we could cover the walls of our homes with similar marks of our gratitude for blessings received. Some of these could read, "for our first born child," "for healing from pneumonia", "for rescue from a financial crisis", or "an escape from addiction to drugs." What a blessed home we would have! God would look down from Heaven and say, *"There is a house of gratitude. I will bless it in a hundred different ways because grateful people live within it."*

The new curtains in my kitchen have a colorful design on the bottom, shown with a loaf of bread and a pitcher of milk and the words, "Give us this day our daily bread." As I sit eating my meals just a few feet away, these words cry out to me, "Be conscious of where your food comes from. Give thanks!" Perhaps, our meal prayers have fallen by the wayside. Be a prophet in your home! God takes on a more precious relationship when we express gratitude for all the gifts of life.

What pleasant sounding words, *"merci,"* and *"thanks."* Use them often in your daily living, especially to those who serve; doctors, waitresses, nurses, and store clerks. My favorite prayer of gratitude is, *"Thank You, Lord,"* even when I make a good shot in golf (Although I didn't say it often the last time I played!). Grateful people bring happiness into their lives by recognizing the number of blessings all around them. Thanks for this day, my family, my friends, and my health!

On one occasion, Jesus gave perfect health to ten unclean lepers! Only one of them came back to thank Him, while the other nine forgot His kindness. Will we take His graciousness for granted?

Make this forthcoming Thanksgiving Day truly a memorable one for all at home! In a family group, attend Mass and offer the perfect prayer of thanksgiving. A Happy Thanksgiving!

In A Cathedral In Florence, Italy

The Cathedral of St. Mary of the Fields in Florence, Italy, with its colored exterior brick, stands out as an architectural gem in that center of art and culture. One warm fall afternoon, I stepped into its cool interior to view its beauty and enjoy its silence.

Directly behind the altar hung a giant sized painting of the Last Supper. Suddenly, the Cathedral organist began playing his original music on only four notes. We call this improvising. The virtuoso moved up and down the musical scale in different keys, and filled the great Cathedral with soul stirring chords of music, first thunderous, then faint.

"How can all this glorious music come from only four notes," I asked myself. As never before, my spirit sang out in joy at this unexpected musical treat which went on for an hour.

As I sat looking at the painting of the Last Supper, I kept thinking of the words Jesus spoke on the night before He died. That evening, on two occasions, He spoke the words, *"This is My Body"* and *"This is My Blood."* Were any more inspiring words ever spoken on this earth?

I connected those four words with the powerful music being played on just four notes in the cathedral that afternoon. I pictured in my mind's eye all the priests down through the centuries and how they have said those sacred words in small chapels, in grand basilicas, on fenders of Jeeps in wartime, and even in concentration camps.

What a holy concert of music these words of Christ have added to the world. Often, since that time. I have traveled back to this splendid place of worship in Florence. In doing so, I renewed in myself the power, the glory and the majesty of those holy words spoken by the Lord at the Last Supper.

As we attend Mass, listen carefully for those beautiful words of Consecration which bring the Lord down on our altars. Treasure them!

The Famous Basilica of Florence, Italy

Did The Waitress Receive Enough Gratuity

About five years ago, I attended the Funeral Mass of a priest-friend, Fr. Tom Nash, a member of the Augustinian Order. In years past, we met each other while caddying at the same golf course. About five years older then me, I saw in Tom Nash an ideal to be imitated. Pleasant, good natured, friendly, and already then a seminarian studying for the Priesthood, Tom showed that one could enjoy life and still walk in the footsteps of the Lord. We called him *"Darbie"* because he always had his hair combed and wore a clean shirt everyday, along with a sharp crease in his trousers. The name stayed with him until his death which came after a long, painful illness.

Wisdom From the Pulpit

Father Tom went on to do many wonderful things in his Priesthood, especially in the education of young men. At the Funeral Mass, Father Dudley Day mentioned all these character traits of Father Tom, but he ended by saying words that I will never forget. *"If Father Nash dined out, he was always concerned about this matter at the end of the meal. 'Did the waitress receive a sufficient tip, gratuity?'"* A small thing, a reader might say, but to me that insight into Father Tom's way of living summed up his whole outlook on life, *"Be generous to others."* As a caddy, Father Nash had received tips from his players and knew the importance of gratuities being fair and generous.

As we go through life, we can show generosity towards others often. The question we could ask ourselves is, "Did I show enough love towards all whom I met today?" Generosity need not be measured only in terms of money, but rather in frame of mind.

Someone Really Cares For Us

Some years ago, the Sister Principal of Sacred Heart High School for girls, in Mokena, Illinois, asked me to come three days a week to teach religion. During the summer, I obtained a school year book and memorized the names along with the photos of students coming into the 2nd, 3rd and 4th years. In September, on the first day of school, I was able to address the girls passing by with their names. Our names are precious to us. *"Hello, Judy,"*... *"Good to see you, Betty."*

Some came up to me to test my memory. I knew them all. They were amazed that anyone would take all that time to know their names. A relationship of trust can begin when people know each other's name. Jesus, the Good Shepherd, affirmed this belief when He said, *"I know mine and mine know Me."*

Picture the Risen Christ, the Good Shepherd, a name He gave Himself, standing before us. He sees our little congregation, some 40 of us, all strangers to each other. We wonder, *"Are we all blank faces to Him? Perhaps just a series of numbers. Our life stories are mysteries to Him?"*

Suddenly, He begins to walk among us. In an inaudible tone heard only by the person spoken to, Christ whispers to one person, *"Good morning, June, I admire the way you are taking care of your sick mother. Keep on, I am with you."* To another, *"Hello, Bill! Your unemployment will soon come to an end."*

He moves on. *"Good to see you here this morning, Marge. I will support you in your sickness. Have courage!"* The gracious Lord speaks to a man next to her, *"How are you doing, Bob? You may think that I haven't been listening to you in your spirit of depression. I have been standing right behind you, holding you up. You will have happy days soon, believe Me!"* The onlookers see joy and amazement on the faces of those spoken to.

What a different kind of life we would have if we made the Risen Christ, the Good Shepherd, really present in our days. I keep saying to myself, *"Jesus of Nazareth, the Great Prophet, is closer to me than my breathing. He knows me better than I know myself."*

Faith Lights Up The Glory Road

Some years ago, I had an unusual experience in the Holy City of Jerusalem. The Old City rests on the side of a mountain, with the result that all the streets go up or down, with no level ones. One morning, as I was coming out of my residence at the Franciscan Hospice at about 5:00 a.m., I planned to walk to the Church of the Holy Sepulcher. I was to offer Mass on Mt. Calvary, in this ancient Shrine (built by St. Helena around the year 300 A.D.).

I stepped out into complete darkness. Heavy clouds covered the moon. The street lights were turned off. I couldn't see my hands in front of me. Since I had often walked this downhill street, about a block long, with its seven turns, I started off to the

Church. The narrow road had walls rising up at both sides. I kept my hand on the side wall, as I cautiously put my foot ahead of me to catch the beginning of the next step. I made it safely through the seven turns, although the last step almost did me in.

The next morning, the same conditions prevailed. This time I had a small pencil shaped flashlight. Its little beam of light aimed at my feet brought me quickly to Holy Sepulcher Church. What a difference the light made! I couldn't see down the street. I just had enough light to take the next step!

We can compare this walk above to our daily journey in life. The light is the gift of faith we receive in Baptism. As we experience the darkness of our walk on the Glory Road, faith in God helps us to avoid injuries, dangerous spills and despair. Faith lights up the twists and turns. We believe in the presence of the Lord and His constant love abiding with us. Without faith, people move along in hellish darkness, exposed to all kinds of miseries.

Sometimes, this walk takes me to my personal Hill of Calvary. There, I am nailed to my own cross of suffering. By the light faith I believe Jesus promises to support me, to be at my side, and at times carry me on His back. Jesus did not promise to shield us from these painful experiences. The Glory Road is unmapped, at times bringing us to places we never expected to go! At times, not everything will be wonderful!

Pity people without faith! The Pharisees were blind to Christ's love. They did not walk as children of light. They rejected Christ, the light *of the world,* thus sealing their self-destruction. Faith is believing that the Lord is in sovereign control, that He will never desert us in our pain.

A Pastor prayed for a good position in a growing Church where people would like him and his family. His Glory Road led him to Smokey Mountain, a garbage dump outside the city in the Philippine Islands. He and his children scavenge for food, along with 20,000 others. Christ is there with him! He delights!

The Church of all Nations – Gethsemane

Music For All Ages

In Paris, France, the Pere Chaise Cemetery holds the remains of many of France's most famous heroes. One dark, somber All Soul's Day some years ago, I visited this old burial ground. Pere (Father) Chaise, a Jesuit priest, served as confessor for King Louis in the 18th Century.

As I walked along the wet pathways, littered with fallen leaves, I read on the tombstones and the walls of the mausoleums the names of statesmen and women, military heroes, writers, scientists and outstanding people from all walks of life. No one stood at their graves. Silence filled the grounds of the dead. Suddenly, at a bend in the roadway, I saw a crowd of people gathered around one grave. Fresh flowers (the French are devoted to flowers) and many lighted candles completely covered the grave. Curious, I approached and discovered the burial place of Frederick Chopin, the Polish born genius, the composer of piano music.

Chopin left behind music that will live as long as people will inhabit the earth. Bystanders told me that this gathering of Chopin's admirers, complete with bouquets of flowers and lighted candles, go on all year long at his grave. In this way, his devotees honor him for the inspiring music he left behind.

What will we give to the world in the way of music? We may not leave a new composition of notes and melodies as Chopin did, but rather the music of words of kindness and actions. Our thoughtful consideration for the feelings of others creates a certain kind of music, maybe even more inspiring than Chopin's.

Show me a person who consistently practices kindness and I will show you a true musician of the heart. Each one of us can enrich the world by our daily efforts to bolster the morale of others by our pleasant and helpful treatment of them.

No need to envy Chopin. We, too, can create superb music in the world.

The Triumph Of The Human Spirit

Do you think that you could survive in a ghetto block in a suburb of Calcutta, India, along with 50,000 others? Picture the conditions: no toilet facilities, except community outhouses, no running water, only a loose tin covering for a roof, the whole family living in one room, with a wood fire for cooking purposes.

In a best-seller paperback, entitled, *"The City of Joy,"* a noted French writer spelled out the daily activities of these 50,000 men, women, and children. After several years of first-hand contact with these people he choose this title. With just enough food to eat each day, these economically depressed Indians showed a stirring triumph of the human spirit. The French author writes of his constant amazement at the lighthearted, bubbling spirit of joyousness in the lives of these 50,000 human beings, crowded together into this one block. They had no time to wring their hands at their abominable living conditions. Of all different religious faiths, these country people had come to Calcutta to escape starvation. Strangers to each other, they went out of their way to help one another.

After reading the book, I found another reason to say, *"Three cheers for the human spirit, indomitable, unpredictable, amazingly strong and enduring."* Even the smallest children worked along with the adults to provide for their families. A rickshaw puller had an average life span of 7 years, after which, his lungs burst.

The human spirit can rise to unbelievable heights in terms of gratitude to God, self sacrificing love and the joyful acceptances of the problems of life. If Americans grow *"smug"* from the *"good life,"* and put God aside as unnecessary, we could end up in tragic selfishness.

We ask ourselves difficult questions. At what stage of growth is our human spirit? What sense of joyousness rules our lives? My visit to India confirms all that the French writer wrote.

Lord, Make Me An Instrument Of Your Peace

In my past years, the story of Jill Jackson has helped me through many dark days. In her childhood, Jill experienced a sad and troubled youth. When Jill was three, her mother died. After that, many foster homes took her in, but none showed her love and interest. In her teen age years, success evaded her in acting and singing careers.

As her marriage fell apart, suicide appeared to be the only way out. Even in this, she failed. In her long recuperation, Jill handed her life over to God, a move that changed her despairing outlook on life. Her second marriage with Sy Miller, a musician, brought her much happiness, as together they composed songs for publication, many of them successful.

One song, with Jill writing the music and Sy composing the music, lay on their piano for some months. By accident, they played it at a seminar and it turned into an immediate success. The title was, *"Let there Be Peace On Earth,"* and it is now sung in 100 different languages by peace groups throughout the world. Who would have thought that this song of peace was composed by a woman like Jill Jackson, with her troubled beginning in life? What great good she is doing!

The story of Jill Jackson should give us a new hope for the future. No situation in life can be so hopeless that we are forced to give up bringing peace into our lives. If we first give our life over to God, we can then fill our days with a peace beyond all understanding.

I remember being in Paris, France, years ago, at a time when my spirits had reached a new low. Weak in health and coming off a troublesome assignment,

I remember praying in the darkness of the Chapel in the Le Foyer Sacerdotal, in these words, *"Lord, please help me in these three H's: Hope, Home, Health."*

The story of Jill Jackson gave me the courage to pray in this way. Months later, back in Chicago, these prayers were answered; a little bungalow as my home, a kind and gracious people raised my hopes for days ahead, and a new spirit of health invigorated me. I experienced a peace of mind and soul like never before. Of all God's Gifts, peace outshines all others. This harmony comes to us when our soul is free from fear, anxiety, sin, unforgiveness and ill will towards God's creatures.

Jill wrote in her famous song, *"Let there be peace on earth and let it begin with me."* Whether poor, sick, or placed low in life, we can bring peace into our lives! Avoid arguments! Even in the family, sharp words can be returned with soft words. Disagree in an agreeable way! Put the word peace on the refrigerator door!

Follow Me

In past weeks, the untimely death of John Denver, composer and ballad singer, has saddened the hearts of his many admirers. Back in 1976, I heard a song entitled, "Follow Me," written and composed by John Denver. The words and the haunting, winsome musical score touched my heart as few songs have in my lifetime. At that time in 1976, I was leaving for Alaska to serve as a missionary among the Eskimos. To me, the words summed up my ideal in the new work I was undertaking.

Used frequently at weddings, the words of "Follow Me" tell of love, faithfulness, and commitment. By putting the words into the mouth of Christ, the song turns into a glorious ballad of invitation to the listener to be a follower of the Lord, His disciple. This is the attitude I took in regard to the song. The following words in italics make up the actual wording of "Follow Me."

In our way of thinking, we should remember that Jesus of Nazareth is saying these words to each one listening. *"It is by far the finest thing I have ever done to be so in love with you for so long a time."* Jesus declares the finest thing He has done in His work as God has been to love me from the first moment of my life. With infinite delight, He has shared in my secret hopes, sorrows and visions of a fulfilled life.

"Follow Me where I go." Walk with Me, the Lord asks, not a mile behind, out of sight, but instead, close to Me, at My side. *"Make a part of you to be a part of Me."* Look upon the human heart as the seat of the precious emotions of love, trust, courage, and faithfulness. Christ desires that I freely offer my heart to Him. He wants to make it a part of His life. *"Follow Me up and down, all the way and*

all around." Follow Me, He begs me, in the bright days, in times of good health and in times of poor health. Stay at My side in all the changing circumstances of life.

"Take My Hand and say, you will follow Me." He offers His nail-pierced hand in friendship. No threatening gestures, only graciousness. *"See, I want to share My life with you, to show you things I've seen."* In these last words, the grand adventure of life, my glorious destiny appears, if I so wish it. By taking the Master's hand I begin to share His life on earth.

If the reader were to hear the music along with the words above, he or she would better realize the beauty of the message. In my time in Alaska, I often played the Ballad of Discipleship, *"Follow Me,"* to help me persevere in my work with the Eskimos of the Diocese of Fairbanks. Little did John Denver know how his work would affect me throughout 1997.

A Man For the Sparrows

Every day, a man stands in front of the Notre Dame Cathedral in Paris and feeds the sparrows. The little birds, called the most common of its kind, about 75 of them, perch in the low lying hedges in the Cathedral Square, waiting for their benefactor. On arriving, he holds up small pieces of bread in his fingers. At one time, 5 or 6 sparrows come to get a morsel of the bread, their wings fluttering wildly.

As one squad receives their little mouthful and flies away, another group takes their place. Crowds of tourists gather to see this enchanting sight, myself among them. Other people hold up bread, but the sparrows do not approach them. In some mysterious way, the sparrows put their trust in this man. Since he appears everyday, they do not fear him.

In the Our Father, we, His little sparrows, ask Our Heavenly Father, *"Give us this day our daily bread."* If this common little creature, the sparrow, can somehow have sense to trust, cannot we human beings, the Father's highest creation, hope fully in His love for us?

In an unusual way, the Father in Heaven provides for the harmless and dependent sparrows. Scripture says that not one of these creatures falls to the ground without the Father knowing of it. The name of each of these tiny things is written in loving heart of God.

In an amazing way, the Father loves each one of us. We are made in God's Image. Our names, too, are written in the great heart of our benefactor, along with our hopes and dreams.

One day, two sparrows were talking to each other about the unhappy faces of the people in their neighborhood. *"Why are they so sad?"* they asked. *"They must not have the loving Father we have."*

Every day, visitors from all over the world throng the aisles of Notre Dame Cathedral in Paris to drink in its beauty and inspiration. If only they realized the fascinating drama that was taking place in the Cathedral Square. God was revealing Himself in the feeding of the sparrows.

A Courageous Crusader For Life

A young friend of mine spends Saturday mornings in front of an abortion clinic on downtown Michigan Avenue, not too far from the Magnificent Mile. In every kind of weather she tries politely to persuade women entering the clinic to stop and think about the consequences of their actions. My friend tells them that there are alternatives to what they are about to do. Two million non-fertile couples had no babies to adopt in 2004.

Recently, this valiant pro-lifer counted 50 to 60 women going through the front doors of this clinic. At most, her little crusade for life meets coldness and indifference, but now and then, some women will stop and listen. The few successes she has will bring my friend back Saturday after Saturday to the Michigan Avenue clinic. Only 55,000 adoptions last year. Yet, there are over 1.5 million abortions every year.

She and her friends celebrate afterwards when a young life is saved. When this courageous young woman tells me of her efforts to save the unborn, I feel a great twinge of conscience. Have I ever accepted an invitation to pray in front of these clinics? No! Have I ever preached a public homily, urging listeners to be active in the Crusade for Life? No! My friend's stories have struck a chord in my heart to do something for the sake of the helpless unborn.

A woman gave birth to five children, several of them with handicaps, several with mental problems. Should she keep the sixth child about to grow in her womb? The mother allowed the child to grow and Ludwig Von Beethoven was born. My favorite composer's music will be played on earth until there is no more time. How his music, his nine symphonies, has enriched my life!

How many Beethovens and Einsteins were prevented from making this world a better place to live in? Will readers take time to pray about their role in saving the unborn in the days ahead? I am going to do something, but I need to pray to know what I will do. I may join my young friend on Saturday mornings.

An interest in the Pro-Life scene will give us a deeper appreciation of our mothers and their courage in giving us the gift of life. One consoling thought for me is that for years, I have mentioned in the Intercession Prayers of every Mass the gift of life for the unborn. There are many ways to help in the crusade for life. Search them out with the help of local Pro-Life people!

Sanctuary For Sale

One afternoon while riding a bus through the bustling streets of Glasgow, Scotland, I noticed an unusual sight. Across the street from me stood a small church, with a peaked roof style and long stained glass windows filling the front wall of the structure. Outside the church hung a "For Sale" sign!

My first emotion was one of sadness. Inside the building it was dark and still. In former days, light had shone through these windows as the faithful had gathered to worship in word and song. Candles had lit up the altar and the scent of flowers and incense had filled the church. Soon this holy place would be sold and used as a shop for selling merchandise.

On the day before, on a busy street in the town of Ayr, 50 miles to the south of Glasgow, I spotted a former church operating as a furniture store. Where people once sang God's praises, customers now discussed prices of beds and tables. This is not just a commentary on religion in Scotland. In Chicago, one will find many churches for sale!

The thought came to me, that a person who gives up the practice of prayer is like a church for sale. Formerly, in his inner sanctuary, this person had reached out for God with words of praise, thanks, and petition. As it were, a light shone out from his spirit!

Tragically, something happened to make this person give up these acts of worship of God. A darkness had come into his spirit along with a deadly stillness. A "For Sale" sign appeared and a former sanctuary of the Lord was put on the market to be sold for a mere pittance.

Our practice of daily communing with God will prevent this tragedy from happening in our lives.

Within us, our spirits glow and throb with light and love as we humbly speak to the Lord through the hours of the day. God, grant that no believer will ever hang a *"For Sale"* sign outside the holy sanctuary of his spirit!

Be conscious of this sacred place within you! Keep only pure, holy, wholesome thoughts in your mind as befitting a church dedicated to God. Seeing those two churches in Scotland, years ago, have stirred up many wonderful ideas in me about the necessity of daily prayer and keeping myself unspotted from the evil of this world!

The Little Way Of Holiness

On October 1, 1997, the Feast Day of St. Therese of the Child Jesus, I offered the Mass in the Monastery of St. John Eudes in Paris, France, her home country. Just a 100 miles away, northwest to Normandy, rests the quiet little town of Lisieux where Sister Therese (1874-1897) lived out her days. On this same day, the Church commemorated the 100th anniversary of her painful death from tuberculosis.

I delighted that morning to be so close to where this astounding story took place. A week before this, our little pilgrim group of four had traveled to Lisieux to pray and show our respect to this saintly young woman. In the mighty Basilica, with seating for 8,000 people, I celebrated Mass at a side altar, on the main floor, with my three friends kneeling close by. Therese said, *"When I die, I will drop roses (favors) from Heaven."* After Mass, I asked for gifts for myself, family, friends, and especially for happy deaths for all of us.

Therese is buried in the Convent of Carmel, about two blocks away from the Basilica. As I sat in the Convent, at her Tomb, I mused that Therese spent seven years of religious life within these plain walls. When she died, the nuns asked, *"What shall we say about Sister Therese? She seemed so ordinary!"* Shortly after her death in 1897, her autobiography, *The Story Of A Soul*, revealed her sanctity. She was canonized in 1925.

What was her secret? In her love for God, she wanted to do great things for Him, but soon realized, in her hidden convent life, the impossibility of such grand accomplishments. *"I will show my love for God by trusting completely and wholeheartedly in Him."* At the age of 15, on a train trip over the Alps Mountains to Rome, the young girl had fallen under the spell of the grandeur and majesty of the Alps. She vowed never again will I fail to trust in God. The wonders of Nature about us impel us to say the same!

Jesus said, *"Be like a child in your journey to the Kingdom!"* In a child's life, trust in its parents stands out above all other qualities. When a child holds on to his mother's hand while crossing a busy street, he has no fears and skips along in a happy way. In all our needs, Jesus wants us to trust in His Heavenly Father's care for us. His eye is on the sparrow. Following this program, Therese hurried along the way of holiness.

Some weeks ago, I wrote a Bulletin article about acceptance. I told how an American, living in Thailand, found the Thai people uncommonly accepting of the hardships of life, with no complaining. With a simple bow of the head, the Thai person went on with life. At that time, I began to *accept* (the key word) whatever came into my life, in imitation of the Thai people and our little Saint Therese. What blessings of peace have poured into my life!

A Pearl Of Great Price

Some 45 years ago, a friend of mine, Father Paul Gilmore, gave me the best material gift I have ever received. One of his hobbies was collecting original oil paintings. One day, he invited me into the attic of our Rectory where he had stored many pieces of art. To my surprise, Father Paul said, *"Choose any piece you wish!"* After much search, I selected an oil painting of Christ. Through the years, wherever I was stationed, my treasured oil painting came with me.

The painting, quite large, measuring three feet by three feet, shows the Lord from His chest up. From the attractive frame of wood, the strong, appealing, bearded face of Jesus of Nazareth, with large, luminous eyes. Tears well up in these eyes, hence, the name of the painting, *"The Sorrowing Christ."* This portrayal of the Lord, by an unknown artist, has helped me realize that the friendship of Christ should rank before all other persons and things in life. These days, as I sit in my rocking chair in my study room, I look into those glowing eyes and share ideas and happenings of the day with Him. His eyes follow me wherever I go. When I walk into my study, I find myself instinctively turning towards His Holy face, a comforting experience.

Often, as I gaze upon His face, I compare my way of living to the way the Lord showed us in the Gospels. If I see a difference between my ideals and His, I resolve to erase those differences and insert His way of living. I don't wish to add to His sorrows by my sins and thereby weaken my friendship with Him. Why are there tears in His eyes? He has given much love and gifts to His people, His friends, and oftentimes He has received back ingratitude, coldness and rejection. To make up for this, I wish to give Him praise, love and thanksgiving

Father Ted Hesburgh of Notre Dame University, often tells the student body, *"Keep the faith and pursue the vision."* What vision do we have in life? Do we seek a bigger house, more salary, a larger car, all good things in themselves? If these make up our vision of life, we fall short of the greater and wider vision we could have! The vision is to seek the close friendship of Jesus of Nazareth!

Make this the pearl of great price that we search for in our days on earth. Avoid sin! Talk and converse with Our Lord. Care for the poor! These are ways to closeness with Him. Look often upon His countenance! Do we have an attractive portrayal of Christ in our homes? One picture is worth a hundred books!

My Gift Of Speech A Priceless Talent

While visiting in Paris, France, I try to stay at the Residence for priests, Le Foyer Sacerdotal, located in the heart of the City with its 40 rooms, dining room, Chapel, and above all, its modest rates. It provides ideal conditions for priests traveling through Paris. The priests of St. John Eudes provide these accommodations with a warm spirit of hospitality. Throughout the seven story building, I see the logo of the Eudists Fathers, and the Hearts of Jesus and Mary overlapping each other.

One rainy evening, at dinner in the *Foyer,* I met a fairly young priest, in his early 40s, with a heavy cross to carry. This Eudist Father had lost his power to speak through a disease of his vocal cords. All we

91

could do was nod our heads to each other. Even now, back in Chicago, when he comes to mind (and I do think of him quite often) I pray for him to have courage under the weight of this distressing cross. Unable to preach and offer public liturgies, he must walk through the valley of death often these days.

All of us enjoy the gift of speech. Unlike brute animals, we possess the means of telling others our thoughts and hopes. Be deprived of this ability to speak even for one day, we then realize what a treasured gift speech is. Generally, we take this God-given talent for granted.

Hopefully, we will use this magnificent power for good. By showing respect to others in the way we address them, by our careful choice of words, we can spread light and love through the world around us. If I talk in a continued, raised, strident tone of voice, I jar on the nerves of all nearby. A pleasant voice adds music to the world and soothes the nerves of listeners. Even in the midst of crises, a cheerful voice works wonders in bringing peace.

The content of words coming from the mouth mean much to success in life. We can listen to ourselves this coming week. We might be in for a surprise. We might have to conclude, *"I'm continually painting a dark picture of life. I seldom say encouraging words to others. I have a strong voice at home, but in Church, I can't go above a whisper in singing God's praises."* Compliments cost us nothing. *"You look beautiful in that dress"* ...*"I love you"*... *"That was a great meal"*... Cherish the power of speech daily, which can bring us true happiness and joy.

Faithful Follower of The Lord Of Divine Mercy

About 15 years ago, on a Sunday morning, I heard a homily at St. Mary of the Angels Church, in the Bayswater district of London, England. My brother, who was with me at the time, and I have cherished the message the priest, Father Michael Hollings, gave that September morning. Just a few days ago, my brother brought up this homily in conversation, as we have often done in past years.

Father Hollings, a friend of mine, spoke from his heart, words like these, *"That homeless man down the street from here, Christ loves him! The beggar, on the street corner, in his dirty clothes, Christ loves him! That woman, a street walker, hopes to make money for food for her children. Christ loves her! Not far from our Church lies a man in the gutter with a wine bottle, Christ loves him!"*

Mere words, like the above, cannot bring out the fervor and fire in the voice of this humble priest, especially when he cried out, *"Christ loves him,"* and *"Christ loves her."* From my friendship with Father Hollings, I knew that he lived what he preached by his help and presence to the down-and-outers in this rough district of London.

I first met this priest in Dublin, Ireland, in 1975, when I attended a three month Ministry Course at Marianella, a Redemptorist House of Theology. Of the 32 lecturers that we listened to, the words of Father Hollings had gripped my heart more than any other. His ideas carried power beyond my understanding, due to his belief in prayer and his love for God's unfortunates.

Much to the dismay of his fellow priests, Father Michael believes in an *"open Rectory,"* one with swinging doors, for the poor, the hungry, and the homeless to enter when they wished. Even at the present time, he invites the destitute to eat at his table every day.

In January of 1993, in Jerusalem, a woman from London told me of her admiration for Father Hollings in his care for the homeless and for victims of AIDS. I said to myself, *"My friend still carries on!"* His secret of continuing this noble work for others lies in his ability to see the spark of Divinity in everyone he meets.

How often he says, *"We come from God's hands as His loving creation, His daughters and sons. His love follows us wherever we go."* May the reader take away some helpful thoughts about one's attitude towards all of God's family.

My Final Homily

In early November, 1995, a classmate of mine, Father Tom Fielding, a good preacher, died after a two day illness. I saw him a few days before his death at a class meeting, apparently in good health and spirits. We miss our friend. I wonder what Father Tom said in his last homily!

If some one would approach me and ask, *"Father, if you had one final homily to give, lasting only three or four minutes, what would you preach about?"* Which of the thousands of homilies I've given would I choose? 1 wouldn't need much time to answer. My last homily would be, *"Jesus is Lord."* Jesus is the Lord of all Creation. No human has ever approached the holiness and attractiveness of the God-Man. To treasure His friendship shows the highest form of wisdom. In my last minutes of preaching on earth, I will cry out to all the people listening, *"Bring this person to the center of your life. This Lord Jesus wants the love and praise of every living human being. We need only to desire to be close to Him and it takes place."*

I would go on, *"No one has ever lived the kind of life He did, in terms of mercy, forgiveness and kindness. By a warm friendship with Him, His ideals of love flow into our being and become a part of us."*

Outside of the Sacraments and the Mass, I found the best way to build up this closeness to the Lord was to take some of His words from the Gospels or the Psalms and use them in prayer through the day. *"Peoples of the earth, recognize the Kingship of Christ."* Leave the Bible open at the Gospel passages, or the Psalms, and in the morning, choose a few Words of Christ to pray about through the day. The Psalms refer often to Christ.

Allow me to give some examples. *"My House is a House of prayer;" "You cannot serve two masters;" "1 thirst (on the cross);" "Could you not watch one hour with Me?"* Now and then, through the day, say the words chosen as a prayer, and maybe add a few words of your own to Christ, such as, *"Yes, Lord, I thirst for holiness of life."* All this might take a matter of seconds, but a marvelous transformation can take place in our lives. The words of Christ take on a familiarity for us. We find it easy to talk with Christ as we share some thoughts with Him about His words...the words we have chosen for the day. Jesus is Lord.

A Vision Of Our Time Greatness

For the first 25 years of my Priesthood, the Archbishop of Chicago assigned me to full time teaching duties, mainly high school boys and girls. Of course, I lived in various parishes and helped out, especially on weekends. I discovered an outstanding characteristic in young people. In general, they lacked self esteem. Many didn't believe in their own self worth. Sad to say, these youngsters oftentimes refused to feel good about themselves.

Because they didn't lead their class in high marks, or star on the sports teams, or make the cheer leading squad, they felt they weren't worth much. This negative outlook on life drove many to a sad, dark, and gloomy way of living by seeking fulfillment in the wrong places, like joining gangs.

St Paul, in First Corinthians vs. 16-18, gives us a vision of our true greatness. *"Your body is a temple of the Holy Spirit."* Yes, this Spirit of Love, the 3rd Person of the Blessed Trinity, lives in our bodies, a bright, shining presence of Holiness. Each one of us is a beautiful, accomplished person, regardless of any earthly accomplishments. The Holy Spirit, whom I picture as a young, loving person deeply interested in my happiness, wishes my friendship!

Grown people, once teenagers, may possibly have brought this poor attitude into adult life. Even now, we may base our self-esteem, and self-worth, on how big our salary is, on what kind of job we have, or perhaps on our personal looks. If any of the above are lacking, this poor belief in our personal self-worth can drive us into low spirits and into doing tragic things.

Think often of this all-powerful person living within us, the Holy Spirit, penetrating every part of our being, listening to our every heart beat. When life presents setbacks, when nothing seems right, we can cry out to this wonderful Friend, so close to us, so attentive to our needs. *"I am Your Temple, Holy Spirit. I am precious to You. Drive out of my mind these despairing ideas."*

Friendship requires sharing on both sides. A friend of mine in Albuquerque, New Mexico sent me some prayers to say to the Holy Spirit. He himself is seeking light for a big decision he must make soon. Here is one I say, *"O Holy Spirit, Love of God, receive me into Your loving charity. Be the master, teacher and tender friend of my soul always. Grant me the power to love You with all my heart, to cleave to You with all my soul, to expend all my energies in serving and loving You and to live only in Your Will."*

The High Road To Adventure

In 1959, at the age of 40, I made my first visit to the Holy City in Jerusalem. At the time, I thought to myself that this would be my first and last trip to this ancient city, over 4,000 years old. Little did I realize that I would be making 19 more visits to Jerusalem, the City of Peace, in the next 40 years. That's an average of one trip every other year. The words of Scripture moved me, *"Seek the Lord while He may be found."*

Jerusalem, the Holy City, has captured my heart. Why? In these sacred environs, Jesus lived, preached and died. We speak of being hooked on drugs, gambling, or alcohol. I am hooked on Jerusalem and the Life of Christ! In every visit to this most interesting city in the world, I offered Mass and prayed in many places where our Savior preached and died for our sakes. The Scriptures came alive for me as never before as I prayed in the Garden of Gethsemane.

I am not pushing for all to board planes for the Mideast. My family keeps telling me, *"You don't have to go to Jerusalem to discover Christ."* This is true! We can find the Lord in our homes, our places of work, our schools, and our friendships with others. The Lord presents Himself to us, especially in the Eucharist and Holy Scripture. As one writer put it, *"The Lord is closer to us than our breathing."*

Always, in coming home to Chicago, I have a burning desire in my heart to tell others about the most fantastic adventure in life, namely to know, love and serve Jesus of Nazareth. In the last 2000 years, He has been the most exciting person ever to walk on this earth. Make Him the central person in your life, ahead of spouse, family and friends! Life will never be the same again!

As we enter the Year 2000, take the Lord's offer of friendship seriously. Refuse to allow Him to be just a plastic figure on a crucifix. Instead, make Christ a living, breathing, exhilarating friend walking at your side. If we have no good image of the Lord in our homes, by all means set one up in a prominent place. Sit or kneel before it! Share our life daily with this friend about our ideals for the day at hand.

The Burning Bush

The burning bush that Moses saw just kept burning and burning. The bush did not extinguish itself. To me, the burning bush stands as a symbol of God's everlasting love for each one of us. His love for us just keeps on and on whether we accept Him or reject Him.

This true story might help us to understand that love better. One night, a fierce fire broke out in a little home where a young mother and her two little girls lived. The mother awoke from sleep and faced a wall of flame between her and the girls' bedroom.

Without hesitating, she stepped through the fire and saved the lives of her children. She paid a dreadful price. The flames scarred her once beautiful face and left it ugly and repulsive looking. People would turn their eyes away when they met her on the street.

Throughout the years, the girls heard often of their mother's sacrifice on the night of the fire. They fell deeper and deeper in love with her and her deformed face.

In His love for us, the Father sent his Son to rescue us from sin. His Son, Jesus of Nazareth, God among us, knew beforehand what sufferings this mission would entail. But, like the young mother in the story above, Jesus stepped through the wall of brutality that faced Him. He did not flinch.

At the Scourging at the pillar, the Roman soldiers struck His face repeatedly in an effort to make Him plead for mercy. Christ was silent. The once handsome face of Christ turned into a bloody caricature of a human appearance. On the Way of the Cross, in His three or more falls, His face smashed into the stony road, adding more fearful bruises to it.

Through this Lent, how wise it would be of us to bring the disfigured face of Jesus to mind. As the children in the story of the fire, told above, came to treasure their mother more and more, so we could do the same for Christ.

Jesus of Nazareth carried out the will of His Father whose love for us never fails. Like the burning bush, this love just keeps burning on and on.

A Two Day Story About $50 Bill

One Saturday, I put a $50 bill into a Salvation Army kettle in front of a supermarket. From my experience as a parish priest, I always found that the Salvation Army gave swift help to the poor and the needy, with no red tape or filling out papers. Later that same day, the mail brought me a letter with a $50 bill in it, a gift from friends. Quite a coincidence, I thought.

On Sunday, the next day, as I prepared to offer the 9:00 a.m. Mass in the Midway Airport Chapel, I put a $50 bill into the collection for Human Development. This special, yearly collection helps needy groups break out of the cycle of poverty. After this Mass, a number of people bought my book of homilies, *"I'll Only Speak For Three Minutes."* One man, Mr. Shu, took 8 books and had me autograph them. In payment, lo and behold, he gave a $50 bill and waved his hand as we tried to give him change. In 14 years of selling the books, no one had ever given a $50 bill in payment.

I am not saying that we should expect a return on some good we do others. Yet sometimes, the Lord shows us He is not outdone in generosity, as in the case above. John Denver, the late, much beloved ballad singer, said that if he had the last loaf of bread in the world, he would share it with others. Share some of your resources with needy brothers and sisters.

An inspired writer once offered an idea. If a family was down to its last dollars, and a part of it is given to some in even greater need, a struggling family is helped. What a thrilling experiment this would be!

In the famous story by Charles Dickens, *The Christmas Carol,* old Scrooge, a miser at the beginning of the tale, changed his way of thinking after three out of this world visits by ghosts. What a joy-filled life became his as he saw the results of his cheerful giving to Tiny Tim's family. Hopefully, we don't need such apparitions to make us generous, gracious followers of the poor Christ.

Meeting Adversity With Christ

The theme of the First Reading and the Gospel was leprosy, the deadly disease of the skin.. For us, in the 21St Century, leprosy can stand for all the sicknesses of body and mind that might befall us, such as cancer, heart disease, depression, and anxiety. The Gospel urges us to believe that Christ is with us in all the happenings of life.

Years ago, an American who had lived in Thailand for ten years wrote an article on the way the people of Thailand, young and old, accept the events of life. Their calm and serene acceptance of difficult situations amazed him. I said to myself, *"George, with Christ at your side, why not have the same acceptance in pain and all kinds of distress."*

Wisdom From the Pulpit

A while ago, I was tested in this resolve. One Friday afternoon, I left my car in the parking lot of our local Adoration Chapel. After some prayer time, I came out to find my little Mercury Topaz, vintage 1992, gone. I notified the police and my insurance agent.

All this time, my prayer was, "I accept, I accept." My mind and heart were untroubled. A wonderful peace filled my being. On Divine Mercy Sunday, two days later, on inspecting the parking lot, there, in all its glory, stood my precious little Topaz, completely untouched. A company had towed it away by mistake. Alleluia!

We, as followers of Christ, can take this attitude of acceptance towards what comes or what might come. *"I accept...I accept."* No matter what sickness, failure, or embarrassment befall us, our spirit will enjoy a quiet, stress free happiness we didn't think possible on this side of Heaven.

Sometimes, when I get up in the morning with a new pain, the thought comes to me, *"This could be cancer.*" Then I laugh out loud. *"Lord, take me today if You wish. I accept, I accept."* Pope John Paul II was an inspiring example in his acceptance of troubling, humbling days.

Graciousness Is Every where

Refuse to give up on the world and the people in it. One of the values of traveling (as a humorist friend says, *"getting out of your zip code"*) gives us an experience of meeting many strangers of different races, cultures and languages. Graciousness is everywhere. I always return home from a trip with my belief in the goodness of my brothers and sisters in the world renewed.

In May of 2005, in Paris, I saw a large number of people waiting to enter a restaurant. Evidently, a good place to eat, I said to myself. The doors opened and everyone took places at the tables. I enjoyed a tasty lunch, topped off with a gourmet, French dessert.

As I began to leave, the woman in charge asked for my ticket. I had stumbled into a luncheon for a social club. The members had tickets bought previously. I tried to offer my money. *"No, no,"* she said, *"we can't take your money,"* along with a warm smile and a blown kiss. I never dress as a priest in traveling. How gracious of her! *Merci beaucoup, Madam!* Many thanks!

Several times, on crowded buses in Paris, women offered their seats to me. In the past I would refuse, but now I sit down. Others will stop to answer my simple (sometimes dumb) questions. Over the years, rarely did anyone show a look of exasperation or impatience at my ignorance of their customs and language.

Yes, graciousness, a spirit of kindness, gentleness, and a willingness to practice self-sacrifice for the good of another, show up everywhere. Christ brought this spirit into the world with His way of life. We, too, want to fill our days with this way of living.

In Paris, I lived with the Redemptorist Community, just 10 minutes away from Notre Dame Cathedral by bus. Of the fifteen priests in the House, only one spoke English, Father Yves, a young man, about 70 years old. I will always remember him for his joviality and friendliness. He reminded me of the old time actor, Guy Kibbe, who was a big help to me.

One gracious person in our household can turn it into a little suburb of Heaven. Be that gracious person, unflustered with mistakes of others, with laughter close to our lips. Be a loving presence to everyone.

What Was In Jeremy's Egg

Jeremy was born with a twisted body, a slow mind and a chronic terminal illness that had been slowly killing him all his young life. Still, his parents had tried to give him a life as normal as possible and had sent him to St. Theresa's Elementary School. At the age of 12, Jeremy was only in Grade 2, seemingly unable to learn. His teacher often became exasperated with him.

He would squirm in his seat, drool and make grunting noises. At other times, he spoke clearly and distinctly. One day the teacher called his parents for a consultation and told them, *"Jeremy really belongs in a special school. It isn't fair to the other children."* As Mrs. Forrester cried softly, her husband spoke, *"There isn't any school of that kind nearby. We know Jeremy likes it here."*

From that day on, Doris Miller, the teacher, tried to ignore Jeremy's noises and his blank stares. One day, he limped to her desk, dragging his bad leg behind him. *"I love you, Miss Miller,"* he exclaimed, loud enough for all the children to hear. Much snickering.

In Spring, Doris told them the story of Easter. She gave each of them an empty plastic egg and told them, *"Take the egg home and bring it back tomorrow with some sign of new life in it."* Had Jeremy understood?

The next morning, 19 children came to school and placed their eggs in the large basket on Doris's desk. In one was a flower, in another, a plastic butterfly, both signs of new life. Doris opened the next egg and she gasped ....it was empty. Surely, it must be Jeremy's. He had not understood her instructions. As not to embarrass Jeremy, she put the egg to the side. Suddenly, Jeremy spoke up, *"Miss Miller, aren't you going to talk about my egg?" "But, your egg is empty,"* Doris replied. He looked into her eyes and said softly, *"Yes, but Jesus' tomb was empty, too."*

Recess came and Doris cried. Three months later, Jeremy died. Those who paid their respects at the funeral home were surprised to see 19 plastic eggs on his casket. All of them were empty.

Learn From The Boomerang

Years ago, I attended a British Open Golf Championship, at venerable St. Andrew's Course on the East coast of Scotland, close to Edinburgh. I remember one precious experience from those four days at St. Andrew's, the birthplace of the game of golf. I call it precious because it affected my life in a positive way.

While waiting for a bus to take me to my residence outside the town of St. Andrew's, I stepped into a small nearby park. A young man was teaching his girlfriend how to throw a boomerang. A boomerang is a piece of mahogany wood, about a foot long, formed in the shape of an S. When the strong, young man threw the boomerang into the air with a mighty thrust of his arm, it made a big arc in the sky and eventually came back to him. The boomerang never failed to return. There is a scientific cause for this.

On that lovely day, in the little park in Scotland, the lesson of this experience popped into my head and has never left it. Here is what came to me: The way I treat others in life will the come back to me, maybe not immediately, but eventually, for certain. It is not a miracle, life just works that way.

Let us always show respect to others. We might well be dealing with angels or the Lord Himself in human form. *"As you do to others, you do to Me,"* Jesus said. Small marks of consideration can work wonders. The smile of a flight attendant or a waitress, has lifted my spirits. I say to myself, "Life is worth living." What we give will certainly return to us. If it's good, good will be returned in unexpected ways. I will not speak of unloving things I might do....Alas!

The Right Words At The Right Time

Recently, a friend gave me an interesting book as a Christmas present, *"The Right Words At The Right Time."* Marlo Thomas, daughter of Danny Thomas, asked 120 famous and near-famous people of our time this question, *"What words spoken to you changed the direction of your life?"* All proceeds from the book go to the benefit of St. Jude Hospital For Children, founded by Danny Thomas, in Memphis, Tennessee.

TV journalist, Tom Brokav, wrote this about himself, *"In high school, I was a go-getter and a top student. Then, at the University of South Dakota, I pursued the easy-going life, just getting by in my studies. I spent most of my time on my social life.*

My girl friend, Meredith, told me, 'Get lost. You have no focus in life'

"One day, in my second year, the Dean of the Political Science Department, a highly regarded scholar, said to me, 'Tom, I have some advice for you. Leave the University immediately. When you have stopped pursuing the dream of wine, women and song, come back to me. Maybe, I can help you.'"

The words shocked Tom as no words ever had before. He left the University and after one year returned, a changed man. He went on to become a famous TV journalist and marry Meredith.

We can apply the theme of this thought-provoking book to our own lives. This morning, maybe some words of the Gospel stood out in our consciousness as never before. *"Mary, you shall conceive and bear a Son and give Him the Name, Jesus."* "Jesus" means Savior, Messiah. These were the most historic words ever said. A Savior was to come to earth, in human form, to save us from our weaknesses.

The realization may strike us that for a long time we have been facing the struggles of life on our own terms and doing poorly. We have a Savior, at the present day, human like ourselves, the friendliest person we will ever meet. This Jesus can enrich our lives as never before by putting in our hearts a yearning for His ideals. These sacred words of the Gospel could change the direction of our lives. Turn daily to Him in prayer for His love and friendship.

The House That Love Built

Just outside the city of London stands a remarkable hospice of 70 beds. Hospice means a resting place for weary travelers. People come here with terminal sicknesses to spend their last weeks in peace. A remarkable place, because the whole building speaks of love, lightheartedness, cheerfulness and sometimes downright gaiety.

While waiting for the Coming of the Lord, these sick people practice caring for each other, and helping one another in every possible way. For this reason, the patients prefer living in open wards with a large number of beds in them so they see each other's needs better.

The hospice staff contribute their joyful spirit and tender care to this uplifting atmosphere. Love, caring and sharing make the big difference for this final coming of Christ to these desperately sick people. At death, at the arrival of the Lord, they hold open their arms and peacefully hand over their lives to Him.

Of course, the patients worked at building up this attitude of willing resignation to the Lord's coming. In our homes, all through the year, caring for each other, and helping one another will set up this perfect atmosphere for Christ's presence among us.

Aren't we all terminally ill in a certain sense? With this loving spirit present in our family life, we will experience a freedom from fear and anxiety much like the atmosphere in the London hospice. Of course, each one in the family must work at building up this caring attitude like the London hospice people. These sick people proved that love can prevail even in the most trying circumstances.

The Miserable Ones

In the year 1845, Victor Hugo wrote his classic novel, *Les Miserables (The Miserable Ones)*. In the opening chapters, I found a never-to-be-forgotten incident about an old and kind Bishop. The story opens in France, in 1754. A French citizen, Jean Valjean, has just served 20 years in the galleys for stealing a loaf of bread for his starving family. To his dismay, he has received a yellow passport from the authorities, a paper meaning a dismissed convict, but a dangerous one.

For several weeks, he goes from town to town, seeking food and a place to sleep. His very appearance frightens everyone, with his long beard, ragged clothing, the wild look in his eyes, and the yellow passport. Finally, one night, in a small community, Jean hears a kind man say, *"Go to that house down the street. The Bishop lives there. He will help you."*

Jean knocks on the door. *"Come in. Come in,"* sounds out the cheery voice of the Bishop. *"We are about to have supper. Sit down, my friend."* The Bishop's sister, the housekeeper, rolls her eyes in fear and unbelief. Jean cannot believe his ears. These are the first kind words he has heard in years. Such silverware and plates, Jean thinks to himself.

During the night, Jean takes the plates and slips out of the house. Towards morning, loud knocks awaken the Bishop, and, in the doorway, stands Jean and the police. *"Your Grace,"* the police say, *"this released convict says that you gave him these silver plates."* *"O yes,"* the Bishop says, *"but he forgot to take the two candlesticks on the mantle place."*

Although the generosity of the Bishop was a complete mystery to Jean, the poor man takes the Bishop's gifts to make a new life for himself. Jean starts a business in a nearby town with the name Monsieur Madeline. In years to come, his charity to the needy and underprivileged knows no bounds. He never forgets the Bishop.

By his charity, the Bishop saved Jean Valjean from a fate worse than death. A spirit of love in a person works wonders in the world. We need more people like the Bishop. We meet people every day, more Jean Valjeans, perhaps not dressed as a convict, but still in need of an encouraging word and help.

St. Vincent De Paul

Sincerely Love Ourselves

A while ago, we read of the tragic deaths of two young men in Chicago, strangers to each other. One man, 18 years old, in a stolen police car, stopped another car on the Expressway and shot down the driver, an innocent man of 25. A few hours later, the 18 year-old killed himself.

Friends of the killer say, *"He was filled with self loathing, hating his addiction to drugs and his aimless way of life."* In final despair, he lashed out at society and then committed suicide.

This spirit of self-hatred has to be the foremost spiritual disease of our nation, driving people of all ages to give up on life. All of us find the seeds of this deadly disease in our own lives to some degree.

Now and then, we hate what we see in ourselves and fall out of love with life by being depressed and bitter towards all close to us.

How often we put ourselves down as being of little value. We can trace most of our unhappy moments back to this self-hatred. The sure cure is found in appreciating ourselves as lovable and loving persons. No matter what mistakes we have made or what failures we have endured, we are still of precious value.

Say often each day, maybe as you look in the mirror, *"I love you. You are a great person. I care tremendously for you."* Remind yourselves of the many good things you have done in the past. Think of your special gifts and talents! Each of us has these.

We will be astonished how this sincere respect for ourselves will bring instant results. A new peace of heart, a renewed spirit of confidence, and a strong desire to reach out to others will come into our lives.

Do we have members of our family in a state of minor depression? Keep telling them how lovable they are, how special their gifts are! A change could take place. When correcting the faults of children, be sure to isolate the fault from the person of the fault. Condemn the fault, but not the person behind the fault. Each one of us is simply great without exception.

The Perfect Echo Chamber

One afternoon, in January of 1995, in the Old City of Jerusalem, I walked alone to the Church of St. Anne. I went to pray for all the Annes I know, but also to enjoy the experience of its perfect echoing qualities. Because of the structure of its high vaulted ceiling, any sound made in the main body of the Church will come back in echo seconds later. Not a miracle, just the result of the laws of nature.

As I sat there in the semi-darkness, a group of German pilgrims were singing a Christmas hymn, listening for the perfect echo after each verse. I couldn't help but think of the words of Jesus, *"In the measure you measure with, will it be measured back to you."* If one cried out in St. Anne's, *"I love you, I forgive you, I will return your hurts with prayers for your success and happiness,"* these same words would echo back into his soul as a healing balm and peace.

Think of the world, the universe, as a perfect echoing chamber! When I nourish ill will, revenge, unforgiveness, I am crying out to the world, at least, to some members of the universe, *"I hate you, I will get even, I will never forgive you."* These curses return in echo into my spirit carrying poison, disease and death! Simply a law of nature!

What wisdom Jesus showed when He preached to His disciples, *"Love your enemies, do good to those who hate you, bless those who curse you, pray for those who maltreat you."* In His love for us, He wanted these expressions of good will to return in perfect echo into our spirits, bringing joy, peace, fulfillment, and spiritual health. "Give and it will be given to you!"

An Overnight In Lourdes 2002

On September 17, 2002, United Airlines Flight #942 landed in Paris, France at the sprawling Charles de Gaulle Airport. Alone, I wanted to make these two weeks ahead a pilgrimage of prayer. As always, I stayed at the St. John Eudes Monastery in the heart of Paris. It has a quiet, peaceful Chapel on the ground floor, an ideal place to pray and offer Mass.

In my plan for the two weeks, I wanted to visit Lourdes, 700 miles to the south of Paris. On Wednesday, September 18th, I boarded France's fastest train, the TGV, for the six hour trip to Lourdes. My Euro Rail pass gave me a comfortable seat in a first class car.

The dreams of the previous months were coming true. I was on my way to Lourdes to strengthen my love for Mary and my Priesthood. Before boarding the long sleek train, I had coffee and rolls in the Montparnasse Station. How delicious this simple meal tasted! I was like a child going to Disneyland with a peace and delight I hadn't felt in a long time.

On arriving in Lourdes at about 1:00 p.m, I walked from the Station to the Grotto, about a half hour trip. I was to walk miles and miles every day in the weeks ahead. St. Savior Hotel, next to the front gate of the Grotto, put me up for the night in a comfortable room.

I spent the afternoon and early evening in prayer at the Grotto where Mary appeared to St. Bernadette in 1858. Thousands of pilgrims prayed with me, the sick and the crippled of all descriptions. A peace and quiet filled the whole area of my soul.

The next morning, I offered Mass in the Church of the Apparitions, just above the Grotto of Mary's appearances to St. Bernadette. What a wonderful experience. During this eleventh visit to Lourdes, Mary heard me say again, "Give me a strong finish in this last stage of my Priesthood."

At noon, on Thursday the TGV train took me back to Paris at blinding speed. I thanked God for making this visit possible.

Our Lady of Lourdes Church in Lourdes, France

A Season Of Great Adventure

"I'm going to make this Lent the best one of my life," I have been saying to myself these days. Maybe it's because of my last pilgrimage to Jerusalem this past January, 1995. Of my 17 trips to the Holy City, my last one turned out to be the most exciting and exhilarating. I was staying by the First Station of the Way of the Cross on the Via Dolorosa (the Sorrowful Way).

Often during my nine day stay, I took a three block walk to the Garden of Gethsemane, at the foot of the Mount of Olives. In the Church, I sat and thought of Jesus sweating Blood on the ground, as He saw all the sins of the times to come. Because of the purple glass windows, a darkness fills the interior of the Church, no matter how bright the sun might be outside. I saw in this gloom the despondency and despair that comes into my spirit when I sin. My prayers begged Christ to give me an aversion to sin! I need this season of Lent, with its prayers and sacrifices, to strengthen my spirit. Sin can easily slip into my life if I do not build up my defenses.

As I look back over my life, I realize that I was the happiest during times of Lent. My extra prayers and little sacrifices, my desire to make myself a better person, brought a supreme peace into my Lenten days.

One morning, I offered Mass in the Chapel of Betrayal, a cave cut out of solid rock, close to the main Church at Gethsemane. Behind the altar was a large oil painting of Christ just after Judas had betrayed Him. I said to myself, *"How sad Jesus looks. Will I, too, betray Him in the days to come? What a tragedy if I carelessly allow sin to enter my life.*" I need Lent to see the beauty of the Life of Christ and grow in love for Him.

My living quarters on the Via Dolorosa were just 100 yards from the Chapel of the Scourging. In the evenings I would sit up and think of the sacred place I was living in. With whips, soldiers turned the back of our Saviour into a bloody welter of flesh and exposed bones, all of this in atonement for the sins of the flesh. St. Paul said, *"The spirit is willing, but the flesh is weak."* As I looked to the Via Dolorosa below, I saw Christ starting His journey to Calvary, holding on to His heavy Cross. From my experience in Jerusalem, I have never quite been the same. Lent will help me be heroic in resisting evil which surrounds me.

The Listener

In my early Seminary days (1938 -1944), in Mundelein, Illinois, I found myself in my room at 7:15 pm every evening of the school year. The rules forbade newspapers, magazines, radios and visiting other rooms. Each room had its own bathroom facilities so I had no excuse to leave it. At breakfast the next morning, we broke silence. Lights out at 9:45 pm, after night prayers in our house Chapel.

The dark silence of the night had its fill of hobgoblins and demons of discouragement and puzzlement about the seminary life. Doctors had told me that my health would keep me from the Priesthood. In my first days there, I put a small image of the Sacred Heart on my desk. For the next six years, this image of Christ would come with me from room to room on the seminary campus. On its back, I wrote, *"I place all my trust in the Sacred Heart of Jesus, now when I need His help more than ever before."*

Every night, I looked at the kind face of Christ, gazing out at me from the image, and shared all my feelings with Him, my fears, frustrations and the loneliness of the room. In the dark corners, all kinds of demons and hobgoblins did their best to demoralize me. *"You will never make it for the next six years! Give up, go home! This life will never bring you happiness!"* The voices screamed.

As I spoke my trust in the Sacred Heart of Christ, a wonderful peace would settle in my troubled heart. The voices from the dark lost their power to influence me. His healing presence came quietly to take away the loneliness of the room. Every night we spoke with each other. I began to look forward to this quiet time together.

In the foreword of his novel, The Listener, Taylor Caldwell, the world-renowned writer, wrote these words,"The most desperate need for people today is for someone to listen to them, not as patients, but as human souls."

Jesus of Nazareth comes into our lives as the man who listens! "Come to Me. All you who are weary and are burdened, and I will refresh you." In all the confusing experiences of life, with their heartaches, disappointments and painful times, Jesus assures us, of His availability at all times, all the days of our lives.

Journaling -A Way To Live Life More Fully

I especially delight in one activity I took up many years ago, the joy of journaling. Putting down my personal thoughts on paper had a wonderful effect in helping me in my struggles to lead a life pleasing to God. Sometimes, only a few words sufficed for my day's thoughts. Journaling made me conscious of my moods and helped me to find ways to master them.

Anything that happens to a person can be grist for the mill, that is, material for the journal. When I heard a stimulating homily at Mass, I entered it into my journal, at home. If I had not written it down, I would have lost this jewel of a thought quickly. In reading my journal in weeks afterwards, I received the benefit of this great homily again and again! Sometimes, I read a striking thought in a book, too good just to read and forget! Again, in a few seconds, this gem goes into my journal, my book of treasures. So easy to do, so worthwhile! During the day, I look forward to writing in my book of life. Sometimes, a conversation with a friend produces a good entry. It might be an encouraging word to me in my low spirits, or an insight into a present, painful situation of mine.

Some days, I may not write anything. Perfectly all right, because I then take away the tension of feeling, *"I must write something!"* As regards notebooks, any kind will do, such as, the spiral type or as for me, personally, I use the 8x14 inch yellow page, legal pad. With all this space, I can make drawings, tape in news clippings or portions of letters. Use different colors of ink if you wish.

Here is an example of the value of an entry I made on July 22, 1996, from the Chicago Tribune.

A woman, survivor of an illness, remembers, *"For a while, I smelled the trees and embraced life. Everything, everyone was special, wonderful. Then, I forgot about it."* The Tribune writer of the article went on to say, *"Real life intrudes. There's laundry. The kids track dirt through the house. The boss is bellowing. The car won't start. The rent is due."* That glorious feeling of that now healthy woman was squelched by the realities of life.

How will that journal entry help me? I was on the sick list for two months during the past summer. On recovering, I smelled the flowers and embraced life. I awoke in the morning with a song on my lips. Everyone was special to me! I want to keep that spirit of delight in living!

The article above, now safely in my journal, will remind me of the pitfalls found in the realities of life! Try journaling! It has fantastic possibilities for enriching one's life!

Make My Heart A Little Bethany

The little community of Bethany, a favorite place of mine in the Jerusalem area, lies just two miles outside the Holy City, to the east of the Mount of Olives. In the time of Jesus, two women, Martha and Mary, offered the hospitality of their home to the young Rabbi from Nazareth. Along with their brother, Lazarus, they rolled out the red carpet to welcome the Lord to their humble home after His long days in Jerusalem.

Although in years gone by I have offered Mass often in the little Church in Bethany, I remember one visit especially, on an intensely cold January morning. After celebrating Mass in this house of prayer, I was hoping to spend some time there in thanksgiving. However, the freezing conditions in the Chapel were forcing me to change my mind, much to my sorrow. When would I be able to come back again to Bethany?

Then lo and behold! True to its reputation for hospitality, Bethany, in the person of a young Franciscan Brother, offered me hot coffee and chunks of fresh bread in the sacristy. A real Godsend! Later, as I sat shivering in the Chapel, he came to me with a small electric heater and plugged it into the wall. With this heat at my feet, I was able to spend much time in this holy place, so dear to the heart of Christ.

That morning, and many times since, I prayed, *"Lord, make my heart a little Bethany where You would be most welcome to come and refresh Yourself."* I asked myself what could make my heart such a place. What would the Lord want to see in my heart as He visited me?

In the silence of the countryside, I heard the answer! To be comfortable, Jesus of Nazareth wants a loving place, filled with good will towards all people, one free of festering hatreds and anger, with no debilitating fears poisoning the atmosphere. I would have to separate myself from any attachment to evil, anything offensive to Him!

Today, Jesus truly wishes to visit us as He did the family at Bethany. Weary from His work in the world where He receives coldness and indifference, the Lord hopes for a cordial welcome from us. Our prayer these days could be the one I prayed in Bethany. *"Lord, make my heart a little Bethany."*

Love God And Our Neighbor

Jesus said, "The greatest Commandment is to love God with all our strength and our neighbor as ourselves." This past October, I spent two weeks in the Old City of Jerusalem, at the Center For Biblical Study, at the 2nd Station of the Cross. While there, I met and talked every day with people from 15 different nations, not in a class, but in casual conversations. All spoke good English.

More than ever, I realized how we, members of the human family, are all children of God. These delightful people had the same desires we have for peace of heart and happiness in their family life. We are alike, our brothers and sisters. I left with many happy memories of them.

Father George McKenna

Every day, here in Midway Airport, people from 30 to 40 nations move through our concourses. Everyone so much like each one of us in that they are hungry for food, tired, and hoping for respect from all. All of us find no problem in caring for these strangers to our community. Most are willing to help if they can. God wants us to love others, no matter what their cultural background or color or nationality is. We can pray for those who lean toward destructive lives.

Our struggles to love our neighbor come in the form of people close to us in everyday life, our next door neighbor, our mean boss, co-workers, possibly from our immediate family, brothers and sisters. We may feel that they have mistreated us in some way. A little corner of our heart is fenced off from the complete love, respect, and care God wants us to have for others.

Up to several years ago, I held grudges against several people. I didn't hate them, but they, in my way of thinking, hadn't treated me fairly. Of course, this didn't add to my happiness. One day, a sudden inspiration came to me. Every morning, when I rose from sleep, I sat on the edge of my bed and prayed for these seven people by name. *"O Lord, bless my friends today! Give them peace of heart, good health and success in their work! I would gladly die for anyone of them."*

Now, my grudges and resentments have disappeared. My health, spiritual and physical, have improved greatly. Has the doctor ever said to us, *"What's eating you?"* The holding back of love and forgiveness can take a toll on our physical bodies.

St. Joseph, A Friend In Needy Times

Some years ago, I flew into Albuquerque, New Mexico, located in the valley of the Rio Grande River. I wanted to visit a lawyer friend of 30 years for a few days. Even a short visit like this convinces one quickly that this land is justly called the Land of Enchantment, with its clean air, its vistas of natural beauty, and a sense of quietness in the air.

Late on the night before I was to return home, I discovered the loss of my airline ticket, the first time ever for me. As always, when in difficulty in traveling, I turned to St. Joseph who has never failed me.

Just outside my bedroom door, in my friend's home, a little statue of St. Joseph stood in a niche in the adobe wall. Before the statue, I prayed, *"St. Joseph, please help me to find my ticket."*

Action must go along with prayer, so I called Southwest Airlines. The young agent answered pleasantly from Chicago, heard my story, took a look at her computer and came back with happy news. She said, *"Someone picked up your ticket on a street in Albuquerque and turned it into the post office. You can claim your ticket at the Airport tomorrow morning. You are really lucky, because this rarely happens."* Thank you, St. Joseph!

I arrived home safely. Once again, my friend, Joseph, had rescued me. One morning at Mass in a nearby parish, my theme was, if you need money, ask Joseph to change sawdust into gold dust. A man in the parish, Art Miller, owned a sawdust factory. All day long he got calls from his friends for loads of sawdust.

I prayed to find my airline ticket. Perhaps, we have lost a more precious part of our life. Somewhere, peace of heart has slipped away from us. Our loving ways, our trust in God have fallen by the wayside.

Pray to Joseph to recover them and other holy possessions. Prayer plus action.

St. Joseph, foster father of the Child Jesus

Pray for us!

Do Not Abandon The Works Of Your Hands (Psalm 138:8)

Recently, while walking through my neighborhood, I came upon an old car with an interesting bumper sticker. *"This is not an abandoned vehicle."* Humorous, yes, but also it sent a clear message to the local police not to tow it away. How wise it would be to have these words printed in big letters on my back or on the parchment of my heart, *"I am not an abandoned person."* No! God watches over me every moment of the day. I am one of His dearest possessions.

This announcement would tell the evil spirits not to take liberties with me no matter how shabby and forlorn I might look and act. When troubles come my way, I would not fall into discouragement and despair. Rather, I would shout out, *"I choose God. I am not an abandoned person."*

I offer this mind-picture, one that has helped me greatly in dealing with hard times. As I sit in a lawn chair, with my head bandaged, my arm in a sling, my leg in a cast, I imagine the three persons of the Trinity standing behind me. (These are make-believe injuries, on my part).

Picture the three persons in any way you wish. I feel Their fingers pressing into my shoulder blades, reassuring me of their presence in my trying times. They have not abandoned me. *"Have courage,"* they say.

When I worked with the Eskimo people in Western Alaska, with Russia only 150 miles away, I thoroughly enjoyed the night hours and the stars. The sky appeared to be a carpet covered with sparkling diamonds. To the north, the Northern Lights, a fantastic miracle of nature, cast rich colors across the whole sky.

Only because of the complete darkness on the ground was I able to see these marvels. So, too, in life, if every day had nothing but sunshine with no dark moments of hardships and sufferings, we would fail to see the beauty and love of God. We would take God for granted. So, draw good out of sufferings. What profit can I take from this new affliction just come upon me?

In 1925, a powerful earthquake devastated the city of Santa Barbara in California. Planners made designs for a new city. Today, Santa Barbara ranks as one the five most beautiful cities in the United States.

Witnesses To Christ

On His return to Heaven, Jesus of Nazareth asked us to be witnesses to His continued presence in the world. We can best be His witnesses by being loving people. When others see us, followers of Christ, as caring and unselfish, they will see the beauty and the goodness of the Lord.

Allow me to tell a story of how one man's attitude of loving and serving has affected my life. One afternoon, I arrived in the town of Lourdes, France, the site of the famous Shrine of Our Lady of Lourdes, at about 1:30 pm.

After getting settled in the St. Savior hotel, which was close to the front gate of the Grotto, I went to the dining room. Lunch was over. *"The cooks have gone home,"* a pleasant waitress told me. I said, *"I just wish soup and bread." "I will tell the manager,"* she said. The manager came.

Andre is about 45 years old, and spoke English well. *"Sit down,"* he said, as he placed me at a table and put a linen napkin in my hands. *"I will heat up the soup we have left over and serve you myself,"* he went on to say. I was not dressed as a priest, just a stranger in travel weary clothes.

In a few minutes, Andre came in with a big pot of delicious soup and basket full of bread. *"Would you like a salad, a coke, or a glass of wine,"* he asked. *"Just water,"* I said. In came a large pitcher of cold water. I filled my bowl five times from the pot, ate all the bread and emptied the pitcher of water. As I was leaving I tried to pay for all this, but Andre said, *"Certainly not."*

Andre was giving witness to me as a serving and hospitable Christ. His loving and generous actions affected me more than ten homilies on the person of Christ. Jesus of Nazareth became more real to me.

Our Attitude Towards Life

One story I heard a long time ago helped me to develop a good attitude towards my precious gift of life. Two wounded soldiers, one a young blind man, occupied the same hospital room. The man with sight lay in his bed next to the window. Each day, the blind veteran, obviously low in spirits, asked his roommate to describe what he saw outside the window. Gifted in the use of words, this man used his talents to bring a picture of the outside world to his depressed friend.

Every day, the narrator described the garden that was next to the hospital, with its various flowers and their colors, the different kinds of birds, and the sky above. These details, day after day, lifted the spirits of the blind and made him want to live.

Unexpectedly, the man at the window died, much to the sorrow of his blind roommate. Another patient took his place. When the blind man asked him to describe what he saw out the window, the man said, *"There is nothing outside the window, just a blank wall."* Of the two men, one saw possible beauty, the other a blank wall.

I wrote these lines in Paris recently as I was looking out of the second floor window of my Residence on a flourishing garden. Before this, a great steel shutter had covered the view, but the nun had raised it in my absence. What a pleasant sight I was missing before all this! When we have a bright attitude towards life, we lift a shutter from our life and enjoy a garden of delight.

We have the choice of seeing the light-filled side of life, the many little beauties of nature, the loving actions of people about us, and the possibilities of greatness in our children and family. I saw a book in the Midway Airport Bookstore entitled, *"Attitude is Everything."* There is much truth in this conclusion.

Our attitude, our outlook on life, can make or break us.

When Captain Eddie Rickenbacher was afloat for some weeks in a rubber boat in the Pacific Ocean with his crew, he kept their hopes alive with his cheerful ways of speaking. *"Help will come. We're going to make it home."* Be such a person in your home!

Who Do You Say I Am

We all remember the tragic shootings some years ago at Columbine High School, in Littleton, Colorado. Two crazed students killed a number of teachers and students. At one point in the shooting spree, one of the gunmen put his pistol to the head of a senior girl and asked, *"Do you believe in Jesus?"* Instinctively, she knew that if she said, *"No, I don't believe in Jesus,"* she would have a chance to save her life. Instead she said, *"I do believe in Jesus."* In a moment, she lay dead, all her future hopes gone.

Jesus stands before us every day and asks, *"Who do you say that I am?"* We say, *"You are the Messiah, the Son of God."* Easy to make this affirmation, but another thing to live it out in our daily lives. Jesus warns us, *"Unless you take up your cross and follow Me, you cannot be My disciple."* The cross speaks of self-sacrifice and suffering.

In life, there are many different kinds of crosses, but we, as followers of Christ, have a common cross, to live out our lives according to His ideals. Within us rages a war, the struggle between good and evil. Every day, we have courageous choices to make if we are to affirm the words we say, *"Yes, Jesus, You are the Messiah, the Son of God."*

Jesus said, "He who loses his life gains it." One writer notes, *"We are never so alive as when we give our lives to others, in other words, when we give ourselves away."* How do we give ourselves away? By offering our love to others.

We can measure our success by living the affirmation we make in the Messiahship of Christ by one question, How much do we love? Love embraces many qualities: patience, kindness, humility, gentleness, and forgiveness. *"If you love Me, keep the Commandments."*

In the Columbine School massacre, the young woman lived only a short time in making her affirmations in the Lord, as the Son of God, only 18 years. We have to do this for 40, 50, or 70 years. Making the right choices doesn't get easier with age.

A Realistic View Of Myself

Once upon a time, a good friend of mine, now deceased, was walking in downtown Chicago. He entered a store with a narrow hallway leading to the front door. My friend was always interested in people so he took an estimation of a man approaching him in the hallway. My friend said to himself, *"With those sagging shoulders and shuffling walk, he looks like an ex-football player out of condition."*

Suddenly, to his embarrassment, he realized he was walking towards a large mirror that was on the front door of the store. The "out of condition football player" was really himself. This incident made him stop and take a serious look at his life style. How good it is for us to take a step aside at times, and review our attitude towards life!

The Gospel today gives us good material for an insight into our attitude towards our weekend Mass and worship of God. In Gospel, Jesus proclaims, for the first time, His Messiahship, using the words of the prophet, Isaiah, *"I have come to offer good news to the poor."* He did all this in His weekly visit to the synagogue. *"These words are fulfilled in Me."* The Nazareth congregation stood stunned. He applied the Scripture to Himself. We can do the same.

Yes, Jesus of Nazareth, despite working miracles all week long, never missed His weekly Sabbath worship in the local synagogues wherever His travels took Him. We question ourselves. Do we look forward with excitement to our Sabbath worship of God, the giver of all good gifts? Or, has this great event turned into a mere routine action, something that has to be done? We can build up our appreciation of our weekly Sabbath Mass if we put our minds to it. Here are some ways to do this:

-Arrive 15 minutes before Mass (Parking will be easy).

-Choose a pew close to the altar (Fewer distractions there).

-Wear our best or near-best clothes (A great happening).

-Take up a Missalette and read the Scripture of the Mass.

God speaks to us through the Scripture. What is God saying to us today in these inspired Words? Build up an expectation that the Mass could profoundly transform our lives if we make extra efforts, such as those noted above.

He Could Only Speak One Word

A blessed happening took place in my life in September, 1934. On the first day of school at Quigley Prep Seminary on the North Side, a young priest, Father John Hayes, came into our classroom to teach us fifteen year old boys Second Year Latin. He not only taught us about Caesar's Gallic War, but also, how to live life in a Christ-like way. Father John never raised his voice or berated anyone in a demeaning way, and best of all, he treated everyone fairly.

In the year before, I had noticed this young priest who had been ordained in 1931, often kneeling in our Seminary Chapel in prayer. I found out, as time went on, that he operated a store on his days off to provide used clothing for the poor. In my boyish way of thinking, Father Hayes went into a special status in my heart. For the last 70 years, he has never left that place in my life. Boyish intuitions often are right on target.

Some years ago, I heard Father Hayes give a homily at the funeral of his classmate, Father Maurice Foley. Then, at the age of 85, still with a youthful way, he mentioned how he often visited Father Foley in the last months before his death. No conversations took place because of the priest's paralyzed condition.

One day, the nurse spoke to Father Hayes. *"Father Foley can speak. He says this one word over and over again, especially at night. He cries out, 'Amen, Amen, Amen.'"* Amen means, *'Let it be, let it be.'* Father Foley's prayer to God was an acceptance of his own suffering.

So, once again, my hero of 70 years had given me an inspiring thought for a Christ-like way of living. If my end brings a long period of pain and suffering,

I will surely remember this homily of Father Hayes. It was the only homily I ever heard him give. I will cry out, *"Amen, Amen, Amen." "Let it be, let it be."*

All priests agree that Father Hayes was one of the greatest priests of the 20th Century in the Archdiocese of Chicago. Remarkable, that as a 14 year old boy, I knew his worth.

The Final Accounting

All Scriptures should remind us of the need to purify our hearts and renew a right spirit within us. A life experience from about 72 years ago comes to my mind as I think of this holy message.

At the age of 16, I worked in the school office of Quigley Seminary to pay for my tuition. Quigley, a day school, offered a five year High School and College Course to prepare students for the Major Seminary and possible Priesthood.

Mr. O'Kelly, the school bookkeeper, with a short stature and crew cut, at about 85 years old, directed my efforts. Quite conscientious and serious minded, his motto was, *"Every penny must be accounted for in the school office."* Every day, in his rich baritone voice, he spoke these words to me, *"We will give an account of every thought, word and deed of ours."* He spoke as if he were a Shakespearian actor on the stage.

Mr. O'Kelly felt death close at hand and trembled at the thought. One day, he died in the school office. A visiting Bishop knelt at his side as he expired. This happened 70 years ago, but his words still continued to ring in my ears, *"We will give an account of every thought, word and deed of ours."*

As the years went on, I came back to Quigley to teach for 19 years. One of my students turned out to be Mr. O'Kelly's grandson, Charles Rubey, a great priest in Chicago today at the Catholic Charities.

I am now Mr. O'Kelly's age and the thought of my impending Judgment makes me shaky. As priests go through Midway Airport, I ask them for Confession. I say to each of them, *"Please forgive all my past sins, those I didn't tell correctly and those I forgot."* Some measure of peace comes.

Perhaps, 40 years from now, some reader of this homily will say, *"Remember the story the priest told about Mr. O'Kelly and his words, 'We will have to give an account of every thought, word and deed of ours.'"* I have never forgotten them, the reader might say. They certainly made a big difference in my life. I am miserly with unkind words and carefully check my thoughts.

Be Kind To One Another

Recently, I brought our Midway Airport Chapel bulletins to our local Office Depot for printing. The usually cheerful, young clerk took them with a troubled, sad face. Suddenly, tears started running down her cheeks. *"People are so rude,"* she exclaimed. Evidently, earlier that morning, a person or two had hurt her feelings with ill-chosen words or actions.

Unfortunately, as an employee of the store, the young clerk could not retaliate with her true feelings. She had to swallow the rudeness or lose her much needed job. As a single mother, raising two adolescent children, she had to allow herself to be the target of unloving people.

Rude people lack self-esteem with an attitude of anger and frustration towards life. Maybe a childhood, empty of much true family love, had crippled their minds and hearts from offering respect to others. They are crying out in their hearts for love while oftentimes trying to destroy the spirit of love in others. There is something cowardly in all this!

These troubled souls resent people with serene and cheerful ways. Sometimes, out of control, rude people will lash out with cutting words and angry looks to rob others of their happy appearances. People in service jobs are helpless to answer back and become prime targets for these predators of the heart.

The women traffic guards at Midway Airport often tell me of the poor treatment they receive from the public. Courtesy, good manners, and mutual respect should mark our present generation different from the Stone Age where force ruled. Consider the words *"thanks"* and *"please"* as keys to the heart of others.

Start off the day with the thought, "I will do my best to help the people I meet today with a kind word, a compliment, or a smile. Everyone crossing my path has crosses to bear, mostly hidden ones. My kindness in word, deed or look may be a vital support to that person in carrying his cross for today."

Be in love with yourself so much that you want to share that love with others. Personally, as night falls, how gracious others were to me that day gives me hope to keep on living.

The Book That Saved My Vocation

In the Major Seminary, a six year course of studies prior to the Priesthood, I found one part of the day's schedule the most challenging of my wish to be a priest. After the big meal of the day at noon, the seminarians went back to their rooms and made ready for our first afternoon class at 1:30 p.m.

Weary from the long morning (we rose at 5:30 a.m.) and the heavy meal at noon, I could barely keep my eyes open. The rules said, *"no sleeping."* I would keep asking myself, do I want to be a priest with all these years ahead of me? How could I go through this lethargy every school day for the next six years? I seriously thought of leaving the seminary. This may sound absurd, but the rules meant everything to me.

Then I came to own a life saving book. This large volume, with many photos in it, told the history of the Missions of the Oblates of Mary Immaculate among the Indians of Northern Canada. Our Cardinal Francis George of Chicago belongs to this Missionary Order.

The book told of the courageous work of the missionaries in the early 1900s in their efforts to bring the Good News of the Gospel to the Indians. I came to know these long bearded men as they lived with the Indians, enduring lice, half cooked food, and the intense cold. What heroes they became to me! I easily shook off my fatigue.

Each school day, at 1:00 p.m., this reading took up a troublesome 25 minutes. Books can save us from giving up hopes for a better way of living. Reading casts a magical spell over the minds and hearts of readers, bringing them into new worlds of interest and adventure.

Draw aside to cozy corners of your home and immerse yourself in books that will change your lives. Make use of the libraries with all their treasures. Share books with friends. Read books every night to your little ones.

Laughter, The Best Medicine Of All

In a special place in my heart, I cherish those men who helped me through the Major Seminary with their wonderful sense of humor. Without their laughter, and their ability to see the light side of happenings, many of us would never have persevered to the end. When I meet these men, now priests, I remind them of their contribution to my Priesthood.

In my last pilgrimage to Jerusalem in October of 2006, I found much inspiration in the laughter of Father Wayne, of Toronto, Canada. I could hear his laugh above all the noise of the dining room, not the laugh of a buffoon or fool, but of one deeply in love with God. Unforgettable! In years gone by, Fr.

Wayne had walked 600 miles, over a month's time, to make the pilgrimage to St. Joseph Compestello. The El Camino walk begins in northern France and ends up in Spain.

Nothing knits families closer together than laughter in the home circle. A good laugh relaxes the whole physical frame of a person. We enjoy meals more in a lighthearted atmosphere where we might share funny stories with each other. Laughter, and a happy-go-lucky spirit, can do wonders for our homes. Most of us are too serious. People in love with God will have laughter close to their lips. The world is mixed up but here in our home we are having a good time together.

A classic story of the healing power of humor...Norman Cousins, an editor of a literary magazine, heard the doctors' report *"You have a 500 to 1 chance to recover from your cancer."* At once, he began a regime of laughter in his days with joke books and film comedies. He beat the cancer.

A sense of humor, a willingness to be a little silly at times can do untold good in easing the pain of living. By joining in laughter, we lose our self consciousness and leave ourselves open to the words and messages of others. Despite the problems and difficulties of living, we feel a greater inner harmony and fall in love with life.

A smile on the face of a family member is like a rainbow in the sky, a promise of much good to come. Be generous with your smiles. A smile says, *"I like you. You are worth something."* In this easy going atmosphere, we make better decisions and inspire each other to a higher style of living. Practice laughing!

The Story Of A Little Boy

Some years ago, I was waiting in the Airport in Shannon, Ireland, for a flight to Chicago. Some Irish social workers approached me with a request. In those days, I always wore my collar. *"Would you escort this little four year old boy to Chicago? His adoptive parents will be waiting for him. They have never seen him."*

The child was crying. Old enough to know that he was leaving his homeland, his friends and the loving people he lived with, he didn't know what reception lie ahead. During the flight, he ran out of tears and ended up with dry sobs. Even the flight attendants could not charm him out of his sadness.

In O'Hare Airport, we walked hand in hand to the waiting area. I could see people with their faces pressed tightly against the windows. Suddenly, we heard wild shouts. The new parents and their group knew that this was their expected child. The little boy's mother swept him off his feet with an immense hug and shouted out her joy. Everyone in the party did the same.

For the first time, the child stopped crying. He realized how welcome he was and what his future would be. I never saw him again. He must be in his 30s now. Infants and little children need love and affection even more than food. Experience has proven that, in places where infants received no hugs and love, the little ones lost their desire to live.

At this Christmastime, the little Child of Bethlehem comes to fill our empty hearts with hope and joy. What kind of reception are we offering Him? Is there a shout of joy these days from our lips as we realize that the Holy Child stands at the door of our heart? Like all little ones, He wants to be swept off His feet and told of our love at His coming.

Be assured, this coming of Our Savior, today, tells a real story. How tragic if we think this is just another boring re-run of an old happening. The little boy in my story brought happiness and a sense of purpose to his new mother and father. The Christ Child can do the same for us.

In these Christmas days, I wrap towels together and imagine that this is the One promised by all the prophets. I hold Him tightly to myself as I walk about the house, sharing my hopes for the New Year with Him.

The Risen Christ - The Encourager

A true story! A young teacher died. At his wake, his students were telling the young widow how her husband had transformed their lives. In frustration, she cried out, *"Why didn't you tell him this while he was still living? He was always down-hearted and despairing about his work as a teacher."* Yes, give flowers to the living people not at their funerals!

The Lord, after His rising from the dead, went about lifting up the spirits of His disciples and friends. He showed Himself to be an encourager without equal. To encourage means to pour new life into the hearts of others. The Loving Christ did not point fingers of blame, especially to His disciples, and ask troublesome questions like, *"Why did you desert Me when I needed you?"* Instead, He wished them peace, with His Love for them showing in all His actions - eating with them, helping them to bring in a record number of fish, and by making a second visit to the Upper Room for the sake of the doubting Thomas. At Eastertime, Our Rabboni wishes us to follow His example and go about encouraging others to live the full life.

In pursuit of this ideal, we need not do grand and glorious things. Simply be gracious, kind, and pleasant to all whom we meet each day, no matter what their appearance or social standing might be. Every person crossing our path has a cross to carry. Our treatment of them might be just what they need that day to continue carrying that cross courageously. All are precious to Christ.

Smiles can work wonders. The smile of a waitress, flight attendant, or sales clerk has lifted me out of doldrums. I would say to myself, *"Cheer up, George, life is worth living."* We can be so miserly with compliments. Humans need them desperately.

Mark Twain said, *"I could live for two months on one compliment."*

Try writing a letter to a friend struggling with the trials of life. A good practice, is to have a stack of *"get well"* messages and envelopes on hand. When was the last time we wrote a few lines of good will to the local priests? They can use them these days. One letter can do wonders for their spirits. Hug your family members! Tell them often, "I think you're great!" One Valentine's day in 8th grade, another student put a little candy heart on my desk, with inscription, "I love you." This memory still lifts my spirits!

Two Cathedrals

One fall day, I drove into Coventry, in northern England, with one goal in mind. I wanted to view the ruins of the Gothic Cathedral bombed out in the air raids of World War II. What a heartrending sight! Only the lower part of the walls of this once magnificent Church had survived the rain of death from the skies. Grass covered what had been the main body of the edifice.

The faithful people of Coventry had responded to this destruction by raising up a new, modern Cathedral on the grounds adjoining the ruins. As I walked through this new light-filled House of God, I admired the faith of the Coventry worshipers in raising another splendid, glowing Temple of Prayer for all to come after them.

During Eastertime, we rejoice that death did not conquer the Lord, the Messiah, on that first Good Friday. All appeared lost, with His body beaten, and bruised, just a shell of a man on the Cross. Christ raised Himself from the tomb into a shining image of hope for all His faithful followers.

Perhaps we find ourselves sitting among the ruins of our lives brought on by our own weaknesses and lack of faith. The story of the two Cathedrals could give us new hope for the future. With the help of the Risen Christ, we can change our death dealing life style into a new and glorious way of life.

Jesus approaches us with His greeting of friendship, *"Peace be with you."* We can step out of the ruins that have been our lives and grasp the hand of the gentle Christ. More than anyone, He wishes to help us build an even greater edifice of our lives, bright and inspiring with prayer and good works of every kind. 1 will never forget Coventry and its two Cathedrals! The memory has often given me new hope for a better and brighter life. Usually, the first step towards a new life is found in Confession.

9th National Catholic Conference Of Airport Chaplains

In April of 1996, 27 deacons, priests and lay persons, associated with Airport Chapels in the United States gathered at the Campion Retreat House, in a suburb of Boston. Archbishop Giovanni Cheli, President of the Pontifical Council for the Pastoral Care of Migrants, had come from Rome to be with us for three days. Bishop James Timlin, of Scranton, Pa., was the liaison person with the National Council of Catholic Bishops. We greet each other as friends. I met Bishop Timlin at their 1995 Conference in Phoenix, Az.

The Retreat House formerly served as the Weston School of Theology, a Major Seminary for Jesuit seminarians of the Eastern Province. Built in 1915, this venerable place housed and educated 200 students a year. With the decrease of vocations, the Jesuit superiors converted the campus to a Retreat House, with a wing of the building set aside for retired and disabled Jesuit brothers and priests. As we ate in the same dining room with these men, I had the chance to meet many of them, a bonus for me. Most of them studied here as seminarians.

I must not forget the Church-Chapel! Since this high-ceilinged Oratory, shaped in the form of a cross, had seating for 400, I could hardly call it a Chapel. Each morning, we gathered here to celebrate the Holy Mysteries with our two Bishops, an experience worth the long flight to Boston. For decades, young men knelt in these pews, preparing for long years of dedicated love to the Master, their eyes fixed on the Sacred Heart, the central devotion of the Jesuits. I could feel within myself the stirrings of desires to be a closer follower of Christ.

Later that week, I decided to make an afternoon of Recollection since we had an open schedule. It was the Feast of St. Mark, I set out to read his whole Gospel at one or two sittings in the holy atmosphere of the Chapel. I pray best when I can walk up and down the aisles. Outside, there was a dark overcast sky, and a chilly wind making sounds in the corners. On the walls of the Church, half way to the ceiling, are written the fruits of the Gifts of the Holy Spirit; charity, joy, peace, patience, goodness, modesty, chastity, and mildness. I spend my entire time, just saying these fruits over and over again to myself, thinking of their meanings! What soul-stirring words!

In the quiet, semi-dark hallways of Campion House, I came upon greater-than-life sized statues of the Sacred Heart. How rewarding I found it to stop and renew my love for Jesus of Nazareth as the Sacred Heart! From the times of St. Ignatius, the Jesuits taught their students total dedication to the Sacred Heart. In Jesus, we find all the fruits of the

Holy Spirit, mentioned above, at work in the patient Christ, the loving Jesus, the good Lord, the Jesus of peace and joy, and the Christ of mildness. If we would set our hearts afire with love for the Sacred Heart, all those fruits of the Spirit would come to ennoble our lives!

The Sign Of The Cross -An Act Of Faith

Listeners can quickly forget the words of speakers and preachers. This is quite normal. An hour after Mass, we might ask ourselves, what did the old priest say at the homily? No answer.   However, a priest always hopes that his homily might touch the heart of someone in a lasting way. So, he keeps trying.

Allow me to tell what happened during a homily I was giving 44 years ago, in 1962, on Holy Trinity Sunday. I was at Our Lady of Knock Parish, in Calumet City, a suburb of Chicago. Holy Trinity Sunday turned out to be a beastly hot day. Our Church had no air-conditioning or fans. As I processed down the main aisle to begin the 12:00

Mass, parishioners were wiping perspiration from their faces.

I shuddered as I thought of my five minute oration they were to suffer through. At the time of the sermon (remember these were Pre-Vatican II days) I made the Sign of the Cross to begin. Suddenly, I saw a young boy, about the age of 7, in the first pew, alone. He made the Sign of the Cross in such a meaningful way, so reverently that I embraced the beauty of this Sign of Faith as never before.

It was as if God had sent me an angel to remind me of the honor and reverence owed to this greeting to God the Father, the Son, and the Holy Spirit. At that moment, I discarded my oration and called the boy to my side. I said to the people that this child had just made the Sign of the Cross so beautifully, that I have made a resolution, in the last few seconds, to imitate him in all my days ahead.

He has agreed to show us how he, day after day, makes this mark of honor and love to God, the

Father, our Creator, God, the Son, our Redeemer and the Holy Spirit, our Sanctifier. The boy then showed the full church how he blessed himself. Despite the heat, all eyes were on the child, maybe an angel.

Our making the Sign of the Cross can be a thrilling proclamation of Faith, instead of just an action without meaning.

Home, A Little Suburb Of Heaven

About 25 years ago, I presided at the wedding of a young couple. In my homily, I came up with an original thought, one that I had never heard before. *"Make your home a little suburb of Heaven,"* I said to them. *"Fill every crack and corner of your home with love, peace and forgiveness, the kind of things we will enjoy in Heaven!"*

A year later, the young woman came back to tell me, *"Father, we have tried our best to make our home a suburb of Heaven."* I still hear from the young woman as she and her husband recently celebrated their 25th wedding anniversary. Evidently, the slogan helped their marriage!

In the planning of a holy family, we should set our sights high. To assume that life in the family has to be a battlefield where everyone fights for his or her rights is to plan for failure. Maybe a childhood in a dysfunctional family has put a spirit of hopelessness in one or both parents. We can't find happiness in family life, they conclude. No, drive out those negative thoughts! Program the mind for a loving home atmosphere where the motto is, "One for all and all for one." Refuse to accept any other kind of home life. Keep asking: is there a better way to live?

Recently, a weekly news magazine listed 17 of the most productive and interesting people of our modern times. In their respective fields of work, medicine, music, computers, architecture, education, to name a few, they will make life different for all of us in the 21st Century. A common trait of these people stands out: they are original thinkers. They work at seeing things differently. How well we could apply this attitude to our family life.

Why accept home conditions as if nothing can be done to better them. If our home life has grown unsatisfactory, lacking joy and producing daily disagreements, we can say, "What can I do to improve this situation?" 20 years ago, over a period of several months, I wrote down 2000 ideas on how to instill life into a parish. I found it to be an amazing experience! Sit down and look at family life! Think up new ideas on how to live.

Put one loving person into the family picture and miracles can happen. Be that loving member of the family! Kindness, gentleness, and humility will turn a home into a little suburb of Heaven. Everyone will begin to think about teamwork.

Is There A Better Way To Do It?

In 1977, over a period of several months, I wrote down 2000 ideas on how to make a parish more useful to the people in the community. I used extra long legal pads with yellow paper and dark ink pens to print my thoughts on how to bring new life into a Catholic parish.

At the end, I had 10 of these pads filled with my illustrations and colorful designs, a treasure house of creative ideas, all of them from my ordinary mind. Many, or most of them, never saw the light of day in the years since they appeared in my notebooks. Great exhilaration came to me in those months of writing, because of my looking at life in a questioning way: *"Is there a better way to do this?"*

Perhaps we find ourselves stuck in a non-productive way of living, angry at the world, a chip on our shoulder, poor self-esteem, gloomy, or despairing about personal problems. All these life styles begin in our thoughts, in our minds, that precious gift from God. To change this destructive outlook on life, we simply need to change our thoughts. It's that simple!

Why go through each day suffering from poor ways of thinking? From early boyhood, I have been haunted with the question, *"Is there a better way to do it?"* In the case just mentioned, *"Is there a better way to live than this way of darkness of spirit, these unloving actions, this dragging of our feet along the road of life?"*

At daily Mass, I hear myself saying these words, *"Jesus said, 'My peace I give you. My peace I leave you!'"* Was Jesus using these words without meaning them? No, He wants us to have a joyful spirit and a sense of fulfillment daily.

Unfortunately, most people forget the power of the mind.

St. Paul said, *"Keep holy, pure, honest, trustful, loving thoughts in your minds."* We are the architects of our own good fortunes or misfortunes. No one can force us to accept any thought. We have the power to say *"No"* to any destructive idea that tries to gain entrance into the inner sanctum of our minds.

The real struggle is not outside ourselves, but inside, in our minds. Ask yourself, *"Is there a better way to live my life? Do I have to argue every day with my family? Is there any cure for my coldness towards God?"* Stock your mind with good ideas!

Father George McKenna

Great Expectations

Many years ago, a short time before Christmas, I was living in the town of Bethel (pop. 3500), in far western Alaska, close to the Bering Sea. Not a single road runs between Bethel and Anchorage, 500 miles away. One windy Saturday night, I left our Rectory at the Immaculate Conception Mission to drive to the town's Community Chapel. The howling, screeching wind made driving our Chevy van extremely difficult.

I arrived early, but found it nearly impossible to coax any heat out of the oil stove. Inside, the temperature almost equaled the outside conditions which were -10 degrees. I pulled the altar close to the stove and put my vestments on over my great fur parka.

That night, my congregation consisted of a young Eskimo mother and her three little boys, ages two, three and four. With breath coming from my lips in clouds, I prayed the simple, touching words of the Mass, *"The Lord be with you....Lift up your hearts...Let us give thanks to the Lord, Our God."* All through the Mass, the youngest child played under the altar, at my feet.

At the words of the Consecration, spoken by an ordinary human being, the Lord, the King of Kings, came down on our poor, rough altar. After my own Communion, I offered this Humble King to the little mother, her face almost hidden in her parka. At the end of Mass, she and her little ones hastened out into the frightful darkness without a word.

Emmanuel, God with us! How consoling and uplifting to have Jesus, the humble, gracious King of Love with us. From His place in Heaven, He heard my words, *"This is My Body...This is My*

Blood," and came down to the vast wilderness of Western Alaska to be with me and the Eskimo family. What faith this little Eskimo mother had to venture out with her little ones on a winter's night, filled with a gale-like wind, to worship the Holy Child.

What message did she receive in her heart that night to bring her to the Christ Child? The shepherds, on the first Christmas night, heard heavenly voices announcing the birth of the Savior. Like the shepherds, the young faith-filled Eskimo returned home, rich with gifts. Treasure the presence of the Child of Bethlehem in our lives. At this Christmas time, leave our warm homes to offer worship in Church.

An Astounding Discovery

Ever thirsty for answers? I traveled to St. Louis to attend a seminar on family life. Dr. James Dobson, a nationally known psychologist on family life, led the meeting for three days. As an aside, I still listen to Dr. Dobson often in his daily radio program entitled, *"Focus On The Family,"* and find it well worth tuning in to. I always learn some helpful things.

In the course of the meetings, the articulate Dr. Dobson stated that the national divorce rate was 1 divorce in every 2 marriages. Now, for the stunning discovery! Then, he went on to say that if husband and wife (or any family group) prayed together consistently, hopefully daily, in a spontaneous way, the divorce rate in that group was 1 in 1100 marriages.

Spontaneous prayers are made up prayers, as opposed to formal prayers like the Hail Mary and the Our Father. Remember there are four kinds of prayers: praise, petition, thanks and sorrow.

In the prayer circle, the mother might say for all to hear, *"Lord, I thank You for helping me today."* The man might say, *"O God, help me to be a loving person."*

In the beginning, the prayer might last only a sentence or two. The people speak their prayers out loud for all to hear. Each one listens to the other. At first, this praying out loud is difficult because people are self conscious about their prayer life. The price of success is to overcome this self consciousness. With a little practice, the process becomes easier and more enjoyable. A sense of togetherness creeps into the household.

In response to the above, some might say this is too simple. However, astounding things happen to a couple or a family group who will give this a good try. The people involved fall more deeply in love with each other. As never before, they see new riches in the personalities of the others. God becomes a real person in the life of the family.

If I lived in a family group and heard of this ratio of 1 divorce in 1100 marriages because of this family prayer, I would cry out the news from the roof tops to my loved ones and friends. I am not discouraging formal prayers. The above is simply another form of prayer.

Jesus Of Nazareth

Jesuit priest, Father William O'Malley, taught religion to high school seniors for twenty years. *"In that time,"* he writes, *"I have read 80,000 pages of student's reflections on God. Recently, one senior summed up what many others have hinted at, by writing, 'I had the assumption that I could treat God like a wimp, as I can do whatever I like. He will forget about it, no matter how I really feel. It's impossible to have a real relationship with a wimpy God.'"*

This poor image of Christ may explain why many, especially young people, turn away from Jesus. They would like a challenge from the Christ of the Gospels, not a Charlie Milquetoast, whom everyone can push around and intimidate.

One of two priests who influenced me the most in my years of Seminary training happened to be a slightly built man, with a low-key personality. When I first met Monsignor Reynold Hillenbrand in September of 1938, he was the Rector of the Major Seminary at Mundelein, Illinois, and just 36 years old.

For the next six years, I came to know him as a person who showed me by his personal example what ideals a priest could have. In preaching he closed his eyes and never raised his voice. We seminarians sat on the edge of our seats so that we wouldn't miss a word he said.

Looking quickly at him, people might have thought the Rector to be a "push over," an easy mark to fool, even wimpy because of his lack of machoism. On the contrary, *"Hilly,"* as we called him, proved himself a strong presence, filled with a fierce determination to spread the Kingdom of God on earth, a person in close union with God through prayer.

People evaluating Christ, could misread His gentleness and kindness as signs of a weakness. In His spirit of forgiveness, they would say that He is a spineless person. How wrong they would be! Christ, with His low-key style, and soft spoken manner, can drastically alter the life of anyone who gives time to Him.

As no else did, *"Hilly,"* deceased since 1979, influenced the hearts of hundreds of priests, because of his rich prayer life. I have thought of him often since 1938.

Nazareth – The Basilica of the Annunciation

The Power Of Books

Books and the written word have unbelievable power to shape our thinking and our lives. As a boy (in days of no radio or TV), I found much delight in reading simple books about boys my own age. A favorite author of mine, Father Francis Finn S.J., introduced me to Tom Playfair, Harry Dee, and Percy Wynn, all boys with high Christian ideals.

My love for reading carried into my Priesthood. As Spiritual Director for First Year boys at Quigley Prep Seminary, I was determined to provide books to inspire them. The school library did not have books suitable for 14 and 15 year old boys. Yet my belief in the value of one good book had consumed me. I began a library for the boys by leaving books in the back pews of the Quigley Chapel. We used a simple system. *"Just take a book and be sure to return it."* Soon I bought up books everywhere and numbered them. Soon the total came to 3500 in the pews and in circulation. *"Return to Me Soon,"* was the motto of our honor system.

During the summer months, the boys could write me and request books from my title listings. I would mail the books to them. With the passing of the years, many of my former *"boys"*, now priests and Bishops, told me of the value of my unsystematic library.

What lessons can we learn from my experience with books? Refuse to give up on books for the sake of TV programs. Even a few minutes of book reading before we go to work or start the housework can shape our thinking for the day. The written word has almost supernatural powers to lead us into reflecting on God.

The local libraries contain treasure houses of wisdom and mind-broadening ideas. I never feel so much contentment as when I settle myself in at the Oak Lawn Library at a second floor table. I look out through the spacious windows at the trees and lawns. It may be raining or snowing outside, but there, inside, all is peaceful, quiet and warm. With books and magazines piled high on the table, I ask myself what shall I learn today? Readers are leaders.

Prayer -The Greatest Experience Of All

In 1932, in the midst of the Great Depression, I had a job carrying golf bags for golfers at the Westgate Valley Golf Club in Palos Heights. Some of these bags stood taller than I did. The money I earned provided food for the family.

One early morning, I got a job toting a bag for Father Eugene O'Malley, the Director of the then-famous Paulist Boys' Choir. I was delighted with the certainty that I would bring money home that evening, something like a dollar. I felt lighthearted and grateful to God.

My mother made me mindful of God as she sent me, at the age of 12, out those 8 miles to the Golf

Course. At the door, she would say, *"Now, bless yourself and ask God to take care of you."*

As I walked down the first hole, I would thank God for getting me this early morning job. My words were louder than I thought, because Father O'Malley, walking behind me said, *"Caddy, are you talking to yourself?"* I mumbled some answer to this kind priest.

The memory of this incident that occured some 73 years ago, has given me much consolation. It reminds me that I did see a lot of meaning in conversing with God about ordinary things at that early age.

As my life draws to an end, I would say that prayer, conversation with God, has provided the greatest enjoyment in my time on earth. With God forever listening and infinitely patient, I have tried to share my daily happenings with Him.

In sad times, in times of temptation to give up on God and His Commandments, in desperate days of fear and discouragement, and in lonely dark nights of the soul, I always found God ready to support me with His strength and love.

In His goodness, God could not have given us a more precious gift than the power to lift up our minds and hearts to Him in prayer. The extent to which we use this gift will be the measure of our delight and joy in loving God.

We Need God

Christ healed ten lepers and only one came back to thank Him. In human terms, the Lord felt this ingratitude. We owe God homage and recognition. We need God. Yet, God does not need us. Many people today admit that God exists and then they treat Him with indifference. Their cry is, *"We can live without You."* Then they wonder, "W*hy are our lives in such disarray, filled with so much sadness and depression, with so little true love for each other?"*

Some years ago, a man named Bill Wilson started the famous AA program to help people fight their addiction to alcohol. AA stands for Alcoholics Anonymous. It is one of the most successful programs in helping people who struggle with this disease. Bill, to all appearances, looked like a hopeless case. Never give up on a family member or friend. Get them to AA.

The program has 12 steps. The first step is to recognize a Higher Power in your life. The second step is to acknowledge your total need of this Higher Power.

Beginning with these two steps, countless former addicts keep their desire for alcohol under control. The weekly AA meetings emphasize these two steps. The members of AA show a truly Christian concern for each other in these meetings. As each tells his or her story, the listeners offer words of encouragement and guidance.

In life, even though we are not necessarily alcoholics, we can use these first two steps to bring peace and harmony into our lives. First, we acknowledge God's rightful place in our lives. We do this by offering God public worship on Sundays. Second, we acknowledge our total need for God's help to conquer our inclinations to evil. This we do through daily prayer.

Everyone, even family and friends, had given up on Bill Wilson, and had tried every means to get him on his feet, but had no success until he turned to God.

Jesus, A Sharer In Our Earthly Fortunes

One rainy, bone-chilling morning many years ago, in January, I boarded a bus in Jerusalem for Bethlehem, some five miles away. Besides my wish to offer Mass at the Grotto of the Nativity, I wanted to view a movie, *"The Life Of Christ,"* in the Bethlehem theater.

As the movie began, only two of us were in attendance. The other person sat in front row with his backpack at his side. One with a backpack doesn't frequent a Hilton four star hotel. He sleeps often under the stars or wherever he can lay his head. This sounds like the life that Christ led. Maybe he was Christ, there to teach me a lesson. At intermission, the employees served us hot tea. To my surprise, the young man came from the front and shared his little box of treasured cookies, bought from his meager funds. I will never forget this gracious act of sharing.

The whole point of the movie we were viewing highlighted the sharing spirit of Christ. This wish to share in our human life began right here in this little town of Bethlehem with His birth as a child of Mary. He desperately wanted to be like us in every way, with all our human limitations, hunger, thirst, and a desire to be loved.

In His Baptism by John the Baptist, Jesus further humbled Himself since baptism was reserved for sinners. In view of a great crowd of people, Christ received John's pouring of water. In our daily life, we can imitate our Humble Christ by being blessed with a desire to share with others our little treasures of food, money, ideas, encouragement and good will.

Recently, I was waiting in line at the Midway Airport Food Court to order a gyros and fries. The woman in front of me had a bill for $5.17 with only $5.00 in her hand. With all her baggage, she looked dismayed while searching for change. I then handed over a quarter to cover the 17 cents for her. Her eyes spoke volumes of gratitude, almost as if I had given $17.00. *"It was only 17 cents,"* I said to her. She replied, *"Yes, but, it meant very much to me."* She won't forget me. Be a sharer each day!

Jesus, The Friend of Losers

On February 27, 1999, a priest friend of mine, Father Tom Donlan O.P., died unexpectedly in Paris at the age of 82. As a Fullbright Scholar, in his youth, Father Tom studied in Paris and fell in love with the city, much as I have in my lifetime. I first met my friend a short time ago, in November, 1998, while we were on retreat together in Mundelein, Illinois.

Father Tom liked my book, *"I'll Only Speak For Three Minutes!"* Of my 37 homilies in the book, he enjoyed most of all the one entitled, *"Serve God While There Is Yet Time."* Little did my friend realize that he only had four months left in life to serve God. Despite Father Tom's towering intellect, he had set out early in life to befriend life's losers. After I autographed the copy of my book I gave him, he sent it to a young Asian man serving a life term in the Pontiac Penitentiary. Through my friend's encouragement, this man in prison had turned his life around.

In the Gospel story (John 4:5-42), Jesus meets a Samaritan woman (a non-Jewess) at Jacob's well, a real loser in life, with a history of five husbands. Like Father Donlan, Jesus was only concerned with how to help this woman put the pieces of her life together again. Our gentle Lord won the day with His kindness and winning spirit of friendliness. Father Tom was much like Jesus in meeting people. Somehow, I felt welcomed and accepted from the first moment I met him. I, myself, being a loser in many ways, enjoyed the warmth of his greetings. Since then, I determined to drop some of my weaknesses and be a better person.

For all of us, we can go to Christ with no hesitancy, knowing that we will receive a warm welcome and a firm handclasp. His warmth, His smile can melt any coldness in our hearts towards life and God. Are we unwilling to change our lifestyle, one that is pulling us away from God? Are we stuck in a rut of indifference towards our family responsibilities? We can pour out our hearts to this same Jesus, the Holy One that the Samaritan woman met when she went to Jacob's well for water. How delighted He would be to help us rise above our failing lifestyles. In no way would He demean us with criticism and scornful looks.

I have lost my friend, but his memory will always stay with me. He was scheduled to give the Priests' Retreat at Mundelein recently. Of course, I had signed up for it. If a human being can make such an impression in my life, imagine what Jesus of Nazareth can do if I go to Him.

Brothers In Christ

Often at the weekend Masses in Chicago's Midway Airport, I concelebrate the Mass. This means that other priests stand with me at the altar. I look about myself in a loving way, and see many other priests gathered close to me... my 22 deceased classmates. All lived, worked and died in the active Priesthood.

In their pure white robes and stoles, these old friends stand with hands reverently folded and eyes cast down. They look on the Lord face to face, as St. Paul wrote, *"We shall see Him as He is."* I recognize them all...Bruno, Jim, Pete, and the three Toms.

In September of 1933, over 250 eighth grade graduates came to Quigley Prep Seminary, located near Holy Name Cathedral. We were all strangers to each other and from different parts of the Chicagoland area. On the first day, the teachers announced that 10% of us would reach the Priesthood. Each one of us was determined to be in that 10%. For the five years at Quigley, and six years at Major Seminary in Mundelein, we sat in the same classrooms, ate, prayed and recreated together. Our friendships deepened as our numbers dwindled from year to year, with 25 of our original Quigley Freshman class being ordained to Priesthood in 1944. We picked up eight other candidates along the way. From many backgrounds, we, nonetheless, blended together to make our lives harmonious and truly happy. We wished good things for each other as we picked out a different classmate each day for special prayers to God.

Through God's mysterious Love, He has sent these life long friends to be with me as I celebrate

Mass in our little Midway Airport Chapel at the crossroads of America. Ever loyal to bonds of friendship, they come to encourage me to hold out to the end. *"George, it's worth all the struggles. We look forward to welcoming you to Heaven."* What a consoling presence!

In our last year in the Major Seminary, in the Chapel of the Sacred Orders Building, the words of St. Paul, written on the sanctuary wall, stared us in the face, day after day, *"Caritas Christi urget nos,"* (Our love for Christ pushes us on). My 22 "concelebrants" never forgot those words in the many challenges they met in the Priesthood before death. Their love for Christ kept them faithful until the end. What about the remaining 11 members of the Class of 1944? All, yes all, are alive and working in the active Priesthood.

So, as we hurry towards a new Church Year, I plan to keep those words before me ...My love for Christ urges me forward. I will do my utmost to walk in His footsteps with the little time left me. My

22 Heavenly classmates will encourage me every step of the way. Readers, do the same!

Father George McKenna

A Sojourn in Paris 2002

On Friday, September 20, 2002, I left the Foyer St. John Eudes, my residence in Paris, after a continental breakfast, supplemented with my own cereal, bananas, milk and cheese. The Paris subway, the Metro, just a short block away, took me to the Rue de Sevres to the Church of St. Vincent de Paul. In previous months, I had prayed daily to this Saint to make my trip possible. His image hangs over my kitchen sink.

I had promised him that I would visit his burial place in the St. Vincent de Paul Church on the Rue de Sevres and honor him with prayer. His body rests in a glass coffin high above the main altar. What a great priest he showed himself to be, spending most of his life in Paris with the poor, and the outcasts, and the orphans. My prayer to Vincent, *"Raise up priests like yourself, so gracious, so kind, so humble."*

A short distance away, on the Rue de Sevres, in the business district, stands St. Ignatius Church, one I always enjoy visiting. Mass was just beginning in this truly awe-inspiring Gothic Church. How gratifying and consoling to join with the large number of faith-filled people in celebrating the Holy Mysteries of our Faith in a faraway city!

Later that day, I walked to Notre Dame Cathedral, which is my favorite place in Paris, its foremost tourist attraction, always crowded with visitors from all parts of the world. I was to spend many hours inside its holy space in days ahead. This day, at the altar of the Blessed Sacrament, peace filled my soul as never before. I could sit there as long as I wished without having to rush off to some duty.

The famous statue of Our Lady, next to the Main Altar of the Cathedral, has always attracted me as she holds on tightly to her little child. At her feet, a new strength comes into my being, a new sense of peace, knowing that she is my loving mother.

In the neighborhood, the St. Severin Church, built like the Cathedral 800 years ago, still serves as the parish Church for the local people. A visit there this day makes me realize the Catholic faith of the people responsible for this House of Worship. I want that faith, too. An unusual day, filled with adventure!

Paris 2002

On Sunday, September 22, 2002, I attended the 10:00 A.M. Mass in Notre Dame Cathedral in Paris, always the highlight of my visits to this beautiful city. The surroundings, the soul stirring music of the mighty organ, and the singing gave me the feeling of being in Heaven. In days to come, I would spend many hours in this House of God, dedicated to Mary.

That afternoon, a train brought me to the Cathedral town of Chartres, 75 miles to the south of Paris. Over 800 years old, this immense Cathedral had for many years attracted young people of Paris to come there on pilgrimages. They would walk the 75 miles in five days, singing Marian hymns and attending Mass in wayside Chapels. At Chartres, they left their needs at Mary's feet.

I walked uphill to this marvel of engineering skill, able to be seen from 40 miles away. Being alone, I could sit down in this Cathedral, built in honor of Mary, Notre Dame de Chartres, and stay as long as I wished. Like the young people of old, I left my petitions with this Mother so loved by her children.

On Tuesday, a TGV train took me to a station close to Paray le Monial, about 200 miles south of Paris. In this little backwater town, in 1673, Christ appeared to St. Margaret Mary and asked her to spread devotion to His Sacred Heart. A 45 minute walk brought me to the Chapel of the Apparitions, the Convent of the Visitation Sisters. A French Mass was starting at 11 a.m.

St. Margaret Mary rests in a glass coffin over a side altar. On the back wall of the sanctuary, a huge painting shows Christ hanging on the cross, with a ray of light coming from His heart to St. Margaret Mary below. *"Love is not loved,"* so spoke Francis of Assisi. I spent four hours in the Chapel that afternoon.

At Ordination time, in 1944, I consecrated my days in Priesthood to the Sacred Heart. This was a good chance to renew that dedication. 35 Japanese nuns with white head coverings came in to celebrate Mass with their Japanese priest chaplain. Christ is loved by all nations.

A Day In Paris

On September 25, 2002, I went to the Montmartre District in Paris by Metro. This section of Paris lies on its highest level. At the Abbesses Station, I climbed 150 steps to get to the surface. At every 5th step, I stopped and said a Hail Mary. As I stood there on Montmartre, the whole city of Paris lay before my eyes. Montmartre means *"Mountain of Martyrs."* In the French Revolution, many died for their faith.

On this rainy day, I searched out the Church of St. Peter of Montmartre, over 500 years old. In its silent, dim interior, I was thrilled to kneel at the Blessed Sacrament altar. Within these sacred walls, Saint Ignatius of Loyola (1491-1556) was accustomed to bring his young student, Saint Francis Xavier (1506-1552), to attend Mass. Ignatius, the founder of the Jesuits, was grooming Francis for his missionary work in the Far East. As I sat there, I was hoping to hear things Ignatius spoke to Francis. The hour passed too quickly.

Next door to St. Peter's stands the splendid Basilica of the Sacred Heart (Sacre Couer), built in the early 1920s. In the dim interior, adoration of the Blessed Sacrament goes on throughout the day. On the entire back wall of the sanctuary, a huge painting shows the Christ with His Sacred Heart exposed, as it were, begging for our love.

I spent two hours within this Church of Reparation with my prayer as always, a rededication of my Priesthood to His Sacred Heart. All through my Seminary years, in my darkest hours, I had confided in His Sacred Heart. Now, on this rainy, dark day, I was asking, in this great House of Prayer, that He help me finish the race with my Priesthood intact.

The best gift we can ask of the Sacred Heart is humility. In my long life, the people with the most influence for my good lived humble lives and were kind, gracious, friendly, non-judgmental, and unselfish.

Jesus shows all these characteristics in every page of the Gospels. I left the Basilica with fervent thanks for His gift of faith to me.

Paris – The Basilica of the Sacred Heart

This Way Leads To Happiness

Recently, a fierce fire broke out in the London, England subway system, called the Underground. Some 30 commuters died and others suffered injuries. As smoke first came into the subway, an official came running up to the people, shouting and pointing, *"Go that way! Go that way!"* Many listened and went in the direction indicated. It happened to be the wrong direction, because the commuters headed directly into the center of the smoke and fire, into death and disability.

In the world, at this time, loud voices scream, *"Go this way! Go this way!"* The voices promise self-fulfillment and happiness. Unfortunately, those who go in that way find not peace, but rather grief, sadness, and despair. These voices of the world advocate a way of self indulgence, saying, *"Do whatever pleases you. Get instant satisfaction in alcohol, sex, and drugs. By all means, stay away from the poor and the needy. They will only pull you down."*

In the Gospel of St. Matthew, describing the Last Judgment, the quiet voice of Jesus of Nazareth tries to make Himself heard over the loud, raucous voices of the world. Jesus advises, *"Go this way. Take care of your poor and needy brothers and sisters. What you do to these fringe people of society, you do to Me."* This is the true way to happiness.

Teach children to think of the poor. When they waste food, gently show them the photos of the starving children of Sudan with their bloated stomachs and toothpick arms and legs. Tell the little ones that food is a gift from God.

Families can build a custom of helping the needy by encouraging their children to put a few pennies into the Church's poor boxes every weekend. By doing this, they stay aware of suffering people in the Community. I try often to put something into the poor box. This practice keeps me conscious of others who are short of money and food.

When we lay our heads down on our clean pillows at night, we might whisper a prayer for the homeless, wrapped in newspapers, out in the cold.

"Go my Way," says Jesus of Nazareth.